SLAVERY AND THE AFRICAN AMERICAN STORY

D0956784

SLAVERY AND THE AFRICAN AMERICAN STORY

RACE TO THE TRUTH

Patricia Williams Dockery

CROWN BOOKS FOR YOUNG READERS
NEW YORK

Visit us on the Web! rhcbooks.com

Educators and librarians, for a variety of teaching tools,
visit us at RHTeachersLibrarians.com

Library of Congress Cataloging-in-Publication Data
Names: Williams Dockery, Patricia, author.
Title: Slavery and the African American story / Patricia Williams Dockery.
Description: First edition. | New York: Crown Books for Young Readers,
[2023] | Series: Race to the truth | Includes bibliographical references.
| Audience: Grades 7–9 | Summary: "The true story of Africans and African
Americans in the United States, from their arrival up until 1850"—
Provided by publisher.
Identifiers: LCCN 2022052377 (print) | LCCN 2022052378 (ebook) |
ISBN 978-0-593-48046-5 (trade paperback) | ISBN 978-0-593-48047-2
(library binding) | ISBN 978-0-593-48048-9 (ebook)
Subjects: LCSH: Slavery—United States—History—Juvenile literature. |
African Americans—History—To 1863—Juvenile literature. |
United States—Race relations—History—Juvenile literature.
Classification: LCC E446 .W685 2023 (print) | LCC E446 (ebook) |
DDC 306.3/620973—dc23/eng/20221108

The text of this book is set in 12.5-point Adobe Garamond Pro.
Interior design by Jen Valero

Printed in the United States of America
10 9 8 7 6 5 4 3 2 1
First Edition

This book is dedicated to Saira Rao and Regina Jackson for their courage and willingness to speak truth to power in their anti-racism advocacy, civil rights work, and through the groundbreaking Race2Dinner and Race to the Truth initiatives. Thank you both for including me in this important project.

This book is also dedicated to my wonderful husband, Rudy Dockery Jr., who encouraged me throughout the writing process and continues to love and encourage me to reach for greater heights.

Lastly, this book is dedicated to Septima P. Clark, whose life, light, and life's work inspire me to do this work.

CONTENTS

INTRODUCTION

Chattel slavery: The enslaving and owning of human beings and their offspring as property, subject to being bought, sold, and forced to work without wages. American chattel slavery was different from other types of slavery that existed in many places throughout the world because in most cases, it was permanent. But what made chattel slavery in America unique was that it was exclusively race-based, meaning that only African people and Indigenous people, as well as their descendants, were enslaved.

What if I told you that almost everything you know about slavery is wrong? Or that although the

United States abolished chattel slavery more than a century and a half ago, its long history still affects life in America, from everyday things like what we eat, the music we listen to, the schools we attend, and the books we read in school to big-picture issues like where we live, which Americans have the most wealth, and even how some Americans—namely, people of African descent—are treated by the police?

It's true.

Everywhere you look in the United States today, there are remnants of the transatlantic slave trade, during which between 10 and 12 million captured people from the west coast of Africa (including an area called Senegambia) and West Central areas (such as Angola) were brought to the shores of distant places like Cuba, Barbados, Brazil, and of course early North America, even before there was a country called the United States of America. Of those millions of men, women, and children who were forcibly taken from their native lands, only 3 percent, or roughly 400,000, were bought and sold in port cities throughout the Southern region of our nation. That number may seem small, yet the impact of their enslavement on our country's development and expansion was huge.

The trading records and ship manifests of European slave traders, businessmen, and early explorers help us piece together a complex puzzle of slave

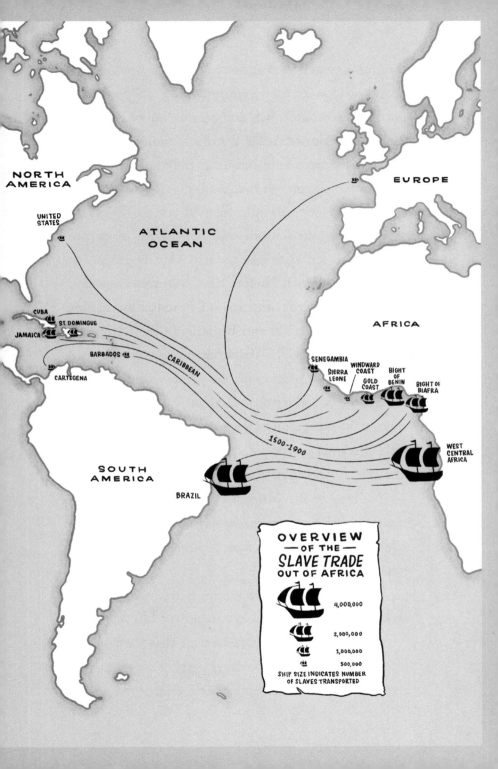

trading that includes various ethnic groups of African people who were captured and transported to slave ports throughout North and South America and the Caribbean. But what slave ledgers cannot tell us is who these people were and, in many cases, who their African American descendants are today.

It would take a while for widespread slavery to take root in our nation, but slavery and its cousin indentured servitude were customary practices on American soil way before the country itself was founded. And seeds of what would eventually become American slavery were germinating in the consciousness and spirits of the Founding Fathers before they penned the Declaration of Independence.

George Washington—the first U.S. president—was a slave owner, and he wasn't alone. In total, there were ten American presidents who owned slaves, some of them while they held the highest office in the land.

You may be thinking: *Why all the fuss about something horrible that happened a long time ago?* Or maybe, *My ancestors were never slaves or never owned slaves, so slavery doesn't concern me.*

Well, the truth of the matter is that while chattel slavery in the United States ended over 150 years ago, African Americans still face barriers that are systemic (meaning they are fundamental parts of our social system). Those barriers include discrimination in housing and employment, inadequate education, persistent racial profiling, and police brutality, which are all lingering remnants of American slave culture. And maybe it's true that your ancestors never owned slaves. Or maybe your Black ancestors were never enslaved by white people. Nevertheless, all Americans today benefit from the brutality and the bounty of American slavery.

For example, slave cultivation of cotton made many American businessmen rich, and not just the slave owners. Business tycoons such as the brothers Henry, Emanuel, and Mayer Lehman maintained a lucrative enterprise as cotton sellers in the South and the North. Their business savvy led to the establishment of the New York Cotton Exchange, which organized the trade of what was at one time America's most coveted commodity: cotton! Before it went bankrupt in 2008, Lehman Brothers was one of the largest investment firms in the world.

Maybe you have seen advertisements featuring a robin's-egg-blue Tiffany box. Today Tiffany is most famous for luxurious diamond jewelry, but it was started by Charles L. Tiffany with seed money from his father's lucrative Connecticut cotton mill, which was run by slave labor.

And you might have seen a suit or a shirt or blouse with the iconic Brooks Brothers label sewn into the back. Founded in 1818, Brooks Brothers has long been known as a go-to place for tailored clothing for professional men and women, but during slavery, it was a popular retailer slave owners used for outfitting their slaves. In fact, Thomas Jefferson is reported to have purchased clothing from the company for the enslaved people living on his Monticello estate. Like some other slave owners, Jefferson dressed his enslaved people in "better" clothing to demonstrate his "good" treatment of the people he owned. We will discuss this Founding Father's views on slavery and his treatment of Sally Hemings, one of his enslaved women, in Chapter 5.

Do you have your own bank account for saving your allowance or money you have received from relatives on your birthday? Well, some of the world's most successful banks have direct ties to slavery. That's right. For example, the global banking and investment giant JPMorgan Chase & Co. was built from slave revenue. Two of the many original banks that merged into the now-huge company, Citizens Bank and Canal Bank, both in Louisiana, accepted enslaved people as collateral on bank loans, which means that if the slave owner failed to repay the loan, the bank would seize the collateral—the enslaved people—in payment. As another example, two of the banks that merged to form Wachovia Bank, which in 2008 was acquired by Wells Fargo, not only accepted enslaved people as payment but actually owned enslaved people as well.

Big insurance companies such as New York Life and Aetna insured enslaved people, which meant that slave owners were reimbursed when their enslaved people died. Today these companies provide insurance coverage and assurance to policyholders seeking protection for their property and families.

So you see, all Americans continue to benefit from slavery whether we want to believe it or not. And since the story of American slavery is about the many important but buried contributions Africans and their African American descendants made to the building of the United States of America *and* about the more well-known contributions of the people who subjugated them, this, dear reader, is *our shared story.*

THE TRANSATLANTIC SLAVE TRADE TRANSPORTED CAPTIVE AFRICANS THROUGHOUT THE AMERICAS

The transatlantic slave trade began in 1526 and lasted until 1867.

By the seventeenth century, "the trade," as it was called by the European elite and slave speculators, was in full swing, with nearly 30,000 kidnapped Africans taken from their homelands per year, bound for life in bondage in the Caribbean, South America, and what would become the United States of America. A century later that number had almost tripled, to 85,000 per year.

Over 90 percent of those stolen Africans ended up in the Caribbean and South America, making them the biggest players in the cultivation and preservation of slave culture in the New World.

As noted above, the North American colonies and later the United States received about 3 percent of all of the trafficked Africans, with the vast majority arriving in the years between 1720 and 1780. Although North America was responsible for a small percentage of the slave trade, it still played a monumental role in the systemic enslavement of African people and their American-born offspring for generations to come.

• • •

Arab Roots in the African Slave Trade

You should know that slavery in Africa started well before the arrival of Europeans.

The transatlantic slave trade and American

chattel slavery are just two devastating contributors to a long history of the enslavement of African people, which began when the Arab Muslim slave trade started many hundreds of years before.

In AD 650, Arabs established large-scale enslavement and transport of East African men and women to the Middle East and India. By the sixteenth century, when Europeans were ramping up their newfound slavery enterprise, the Arabs had already captured and enslaved an estimated 7.25 million African people! Modest estimates suggest that by the nineteenth century, the Arab world was responsible for the enslavement of upward of 10 million Africans, thus setting the stage for the European transatlantic slave trade. What both exploitative enterprises had in common was the quest for riches and raw materials, as well as vast sources of free labor.

In the practice known as the trans-Saharan slave trade, Arab slavers targeted East and West Africa. While the Arab Muslim slave trade did not operate as part of the transatlantic slave trade, it foreshadowed what was to come.

Prior to setting their sights on the African continent for slave labor to build and support culture and life in the Middle East and parts of the

Mediterranean, Arabs had conquered and enslaved the Bosnian people, who were part of an ethnic and linguistic group called Slavs. (In fact, the word *slave* comes from *Slav*.) Today *Slav* refers to the Slavic people of eastern Europe as well as the captivity and enslavement of peoples from that region by the Arab slave traders during the Middle Ages.

DID YOU KNOW THAT THE TERM

slave

ORIGINATED WITH ARAB SLAVE TRADING
IN WHAT IS PRESENT-DAY BOSNIA?

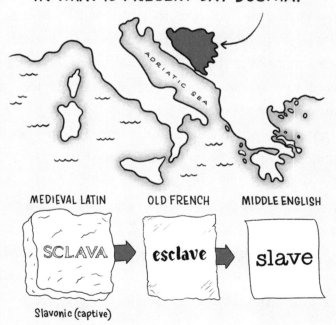

MEDIEVAL LATIN	OLD FRENCH	MIDDLE ENGLISH
SCLAVA	esclave	slave

Slavonic (captive)

What's more important to know is that even today, various forms of slavery remain as thriving and violent businesses in many parts of the world. Many modern-day enslaved people are hidden in plain sight, forced to work in restaurants, in private homes, or in other businesses without pay and against their will.

As recently as 2016, over 500,000 people were documented as living in forced labor in Arab states, including places like Yemen, Syria, and Iraq. Today slavery exists in various forms and can involve international, regional, and local human trafficking of men, women, and children who are forced to work long hours as domestic help or in grueling and dangerous work in fisheries or other industries. Women are often forced into sex work. Children are forced to work long hours as restaurant help and shop clerks. Even here in the United States, human trafficking of men, women, and children is big, bad business.

● ● ●

PEOPLE, PORTALS, AND PASSAGES

The truth is, slavery in the North American colonies grew gradually, becoming more and more useful, profitable, and accepted by white people, who, ironically, had fled oppressive rule of the British monarchy to live freely in the New World.

The story of slavery and the making of the United States is one of people, portals, and passages. It's the story of many people: Africans, Europeans, colonists, the enslaved, politicians, rich people, poor people, Indigenous people, free people of color, the Founding Fathers, your teachers, your parents and grandparents, your distant ancestors, the kid sitting next to you in your social studies class, and YOU! Understanding just what happened during slavery, and what led a burgeoning nation built on the promise of life, liberty, and the pursuit of happiness for its citizenry down such a dark and horrific path is vitally important to ensuring that such injustices never happen again.

It's the story of many different portals—that is, points of entry or exchange. For two centuries, millions of captured Africans spent months trapped in filth and waste, and under the constant threat of physical and sexual abuse at the hands of their captors. In Africa, they were held captive in dark, damp, and disease-ridden "slave castles" that had once served as impenetrable military forts established by Europeans who first pillaged coastal regions of their natural resources—and then turned to human trafficking. That's how the international slave trade began. Captive Africans and their enslaved African American descendants were bought, sold, traded for services and goods, and reduced to nothing more than property: chattel slaves, who could be moved or shipped off at a moment's notice.

The story of slavery and the making of the United States is also a story of passage: the harrowing journey that captive African men, women, and children were forced to endure on their way to an unknown destination surrounded by people who did not even speak their language. The voyages that included the slave trade formed a triangle: Ships carrying manufactured goods, such as guns, cloth, and beer, sailed from Europe to Africa. African kings traded their captured enemies for these goods, and those human captives were shipped to the Americas to be traded for raw materials like sugar, lumber, and furs, which were sent to Europe. The trip from the west coast of Africa to the so-called New World came to be called the Middle Passage. This transatlantic crossing ended at coastal ports like Jamestown, Charleston, and New Orleans, and at Caribbean and South American outposts such as Barbados and Brazil.

But this is also the triumphant story of safe passages

Black people secured for themselves. Take, for instance, the fifteenth- and sixteenth-century seafaring Black men from West Africa who found work as translators and mariners in the early years of the slave trade! Centuries later, in the newly established United States, free Black men would work on the wharves of port cities like Baltimore, making a living alongside immigrant men from places like Ireland. As with much of American history, Black contributions to American maritime culture have been virtually omitted from history books.

The Underground Railroad provided safe passage for desperate runaway enslaved people who sought refuge and freedom in the Northern free states and places as far away as Canada and England. This clandestine system seamlessly moved freedom-seeking enslaved people out of the South, often under the cover of darkness, sometimes hiding them in plain sight using fake freedom papers and creative stories to throw off any suspicion they might arouse.

Several nineteenth-century autobiographies of formerly enslaved people, written in their own words, have been collected in a one-volume edition titled *The Classic Slave Narratives,* edited by Henry Louis Gates Jr. Those narratives provide evidence of the brutal and barbaric culture of American chattel slavery, and the violence and fear enslaved people endured for centuries. Later, we will examine the slave narratives of Frederick Douglass, Olaudah Equiano, and Harriet Jacobs for first-person accounts of their lives as enslaved people as well as the great lengths they went to in gaining their freedom.

These courageous writers used the power of the pen to convince white Northerners that slavery was evil and to persuade them to fight for the abolition of slavery and the freedom of enslaved people as a Christian matter.

And their tactics worked! Their personal stories inspired many white people to take up the twin causes of abolition and emancipation.

Long after slavery ended, oral histories—interviews with people who lived the experiences—recorded the memories of some formerly enslaved people. The interviewees recounted not only the daily horrors of plantation life but also the rich cultural traditions enslaved people developed as a way to maintain community and ultimately to survive their nightmarish existence in bondage. During the early to mid twentieth century, scholars like Zora Neale Hurston, Lorenzo Dow Turner, and Lawrence Levine did research on formerly enslaved people still living in the South by documenting what the survivors remembered about their lives in bondage. These first-person recordings give detailed accounts of slave culture, including the violence, suffering, and fear enslaved people experienced, along with the joy, customs, and traditions they retained from their African roots or developed as survival mechanisms.

The Sankofa bird, a symbol from the Akan people of Ghana, West Africa. It means "looking back to go forward."

Understanding slavery's place in the United States and its impact on American society today means uncovering what's been hidden and shining a light on it.

To understand the enduring effects of slavery on just about every aspect of American society, we have to go back in time. Understanding the past is vital so that we can make meaningful changes today to ensure a brighter and more inclusive future for all people.

If you're ready, let's go back to where it all started.

CHAPTER I

EARLY AFRICAN PRESENCE IN AMERICA

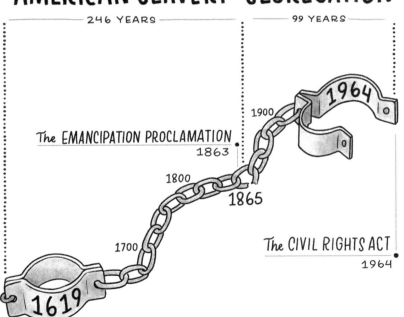

AMERICAN SLAVERY SEGREGATION

—— 246 YEARS ——   —— 99 YEARS ——

1964

1900

The EMANCIPATION PROCLAMATION
1863

1800

1865

1700

The CIVIL RIGHTS ACT
1964

1619

BLACK PEOPLE WERE HERE EVEN BEFORE SLAVERY STARTED IN AMERICA

By most historical accounts, slavery in North America dates from 1619. That's when Virginia's governor, George Yeardley, purchased "20. and odd Negroes" from the crew of an English privateer ship in exchange for food. The governor's purchase of those twenty Africans marked the beginning of two and a half centuries of North American slavery.

But African people had come to the shores of what would become the United States of America well before 1619—some as captured people, some as indentured servants, and others on expeditions, but all alongside European explorers.

The first Africans who came to North America came from Europe, not Africa. They actually accompanied the explorers who "discovered" new lands for the royal monarchies of Spain and Portugal.

Take, for instance, Juan "Handsome John" Garrido, an African conquistador who first accompanied the Spanish explorer Juan Ponce de León to what is now Puerto Rico in 1508 in search of gold, and then in 1513 to what we now know as Florida. Conquistadors were a cross between soldiers and pirates, but instead of conquering and pillaging foreign places for themselves, they did it for the rulers who paid for their voyages.

We can't say for certain just how Handsome John came to be a free African man living among the Portuguese, or how he got his nickname, for that matter! Some historians speculate that he was the son of a king who made special provisions for him to work as a business liaison between the Portuguese and his father. Others say that he had been formerly enslaved but somehow managed to buy or be granted his freedom from his master, Pedro Garrido, a Spaniard who was aboard a vessel in the same convoy that carried Handsome John during his first expedition to the Americas.

What we can say for sure is that Juan Garrido was born in West Africa around 1487 and moved at some point to Lisbon, Portugal. In 1503, at around sixteen years old, he left Lisbon and traveled to Seville, Spain, to embark upon his first maritime adventure to Hispaniola, the island now shared by Haiti and the Dominican Republic.

The men Garrido accompanied to the West Indies island pillaged the land for gold and captured the Indigenous Taino they encountered by orders of the Spanish government in an attempt to spread Catholicism throughout the world.

It might be hard to believe that a man who may have himself been enslaved would invade Native peoples' lands, pillaging and plundering for the glory of Spain and the expansion of Spanish rule, but that just goes to show that everything we know about slavery isn't always black and white.

Five years later, Garrido left Hispaniola alongside Ponce de León in search of gold in what is now known as Puerto Rico. A loyal and trusted companion, Garrido fought to subdue the Taino people in support of Ponce de León, who became governor of the island (though he had no right to do so), on behalf of the Spanish government. The Indigenous people were resilient, however, and fought against the Europeans who had invaded their land.

During that same century there was at least one documented incident involving the transport of captured Africans to what we now recognize as the United States of America. In 1526, slave catchers attempted to transport a shipload of captured Africans to the New World. But their efforts were foiled when the captives revolted and escaped in what today is South Carolina. The captives found themselves thousands of miles away from their native lands, on the distant and unknown shores of America. Little did they know that, in the years to come, many more unsuspecting African men, women, and children would be caught up in a merciless current that would carry them across the Atlantic Ocean, far away from home.

By the middle of the sixteenth century, Africans, both free and enslaved, were being transported to the southern region of North America. In 1565, a Spaniard named Pedro Menéndez de Avilés arrived in what is now Florida, accompanied by free and enslaved Africans who built the first buildings, including a Catholic church, in Saint Augustine, a new settlement established by Menéndez de Avilés on behalf of the Spanish Crown. The African people who supplied Menéndez de Avilés with the labor to build the new Spanish outpost carried out many necessary tasks, from building construction to ironworking to farming. Some of the Africans helped construct Castillo de San Marcos, one of the first masonry forts erected in what is now the continental United States.

Menéndez de Avilés and other Spanish explorers were charged with extending Spanish rule and influence by establishing new territories and converting Indigenous people and free and enslaved Africans alike to Catholicism. By the seventeenth century, Saint Augustine would be a beacon of hope for enslaved people in the nearby Southern colonies. We will learn more about this in Chapter 6.

The Seafaring Black Jacks

Have you heard of the seafaring Black Jacks? You probably haven't. That's because, like much of American history, stories about maritime culture and seafaring adventure center on white men's experiences, omitting the colossal contributions of Black mariners who harnessed their knowledge of oceans and seas for occupation, adventure, and bounty.

Black men from Africa and parts of Europe were traveling by sea throughout the world during the sixteenth century and participated in some of the most significant New World explorations. Others served in support roles, using their linguistic skills in early slave-trading convoys that left the coast of Africa.

Some African and African American men were even pirates or buccaneers during the late seventeenth century!

Later, Black men in the American colonies occupied service roles such as cooks, stewards, drummers, and fifers aboard ships. By the time of the American Revolution, they were thriving as valuable seamen.

But seafaring was a dangerous way for a Black

The Black Jacks crew of the Rathdown, *1892.*

man to earn a living during slavery. Free Black Jacks traveling from the North to Southern states, where slavery was a booming industry, constantly faced threats of jail, kidnapping, and enslavement. Sadly, thousands of seafaring Black men who worked as navigators and as crew members aboard trade ships were sometimes captured and sent into slavery.

Yet others were able to make a living as skilled mariners and businessmen. Some, like Juan Garrido, even amassed wealth and influence as a result of their nautical expeditions.

SIXTEENTH-CENTURY BLACK CONQUISTADORS

In 1513, Garrido accompanied Ponce de León to Florida, but they were no match for the Native people they encountered. They left defeated, and it would be over a decade before Garrido would travel with Ponce de León again. But, in the meantime, he kept very busy as a skilled conquistador.

In 1519, Handsome John helped the Spanish conquistador Hernán Cortés invade the Aztec Empire and claim the area that is now Mexico for Spain. But the Aztec people were a greater military match than Cortés and his men imagined. By the time the conquest was over, a great many Spaniards and Native people had been killed. However, Garrido survived, and as a reward for his valor, he was given land and property near the capital city of Tenochtitlán, where he settled down, married, had three children, and became a farmer.

Garrido returned to Florida in 1521 alongside Ponce de León on what would be the Spanish explorer's last expedition. Armed with weapons, supplies, and men to subdue the Indigenous people they encountered, Ponce de León and his fellow conquistadors were still no match for the Native Americans they tried to conquer. Juan Ponce de León lost his life as a result of an arrow wound during the failed conquest. But once again, Garrido escaped death while fighting for European expansion into North America.

During his lifetime, Handsome John traveled throughout the world as a free Black man who helped the Spaniards invade, pillage, and capture the people they encountered, just as they would go on to do in his native land on the west coast of Africa.

By traveling to the New World—distant lands occupied by diverse Indigenous people—alongside European traders and conquistadors who would stake their claims throughout North and South America and the Caribbean, Garrido, and others like him, helped fuel European expansion and the subsequent widespread theft of natural resources and people from Africa that followed. Ultimately, the explorers didn't discover a "new world." In reality, they only encountered places and people that were unknown or "new" to *them.*

In the next century, European colonies would not only survive but begin to thrive off slave labor during what would become the largest and most lucrative market for the mass enslavement of people in world history.

AFRICAN PEOPLE FROM DIVERSE ETHNIC BACKGROUNDS WERE TARGETED, CAPTURED, AND ENSLAVED BY EUROPEAN SLAVE TRADERS

During the 1400s, European nations set their sights on the natural resources—spices, minerals, and precious metals—found on the continents of Africa and Asia. Seafaring Portuguese explorers and traders first arrived on the west coast of Africa in the fifteenth century. They wanted access to Africa's rich natural sources, such as plentiful gold flowing from the west coast mines in what is now Ghana. Gold was so abundant in Ghana that the Portuguese gave the coastal African region the name Mina to refer to the bountiful gold mines they encountered there; in 1821 it became a British colony named the Gold Coast, and that name stuck until Ghana renamed itself upon independence in 1957. The continent of Africa was appealing to European empires that wanted to amass greater wealth, power, and exclusive trade routes and arrangements with Asia.

Once they arrived in Africa, they encountered people of different ethnic, religious, and linguistic backgrounds. Just as most early European travelers had never seen Black people before they landed upon the shores of Africa, most of the free Africans they met upon arrival had never encountered white men.

By the fifteenth century, Europeans realized that they had struck it rich in Africa! Seeing the vast resources, they began trading with African leaders. Over time, however, Europeans realized the value of Africa's most precious resource—its people.

At first the enterprise of chattel slavery was mutually beneficial for both Europeans and African tribal leaders. Europeans traded items such as cloth, metals, guns, and ammunition for captive Africans who were prisoners of war or who had been kidnapped by other Africans precisely for the purpose of trade with Europeans.

The Portuguese prince Henry the Navigator sent explorers to the west coast of Africa in search of natural riches and access to the region's robust spice trade routes. But by the mid-fifteenth century, Portugal's emissaries returned with gold dust *and* ten captured Africans, who would be the first of millions to be captured, enslaved, and trafficked for four centuries to come. In 1444, the Portuguese captured 240 African men, women, and children from Arguin Island, located near Mauritania. Upon their return to Portugal, they forced their captives to walk naked along the bustling Lisbon trading docks, where curious onlookers witnessed what would be the first of many shipments of human cargo. A decade later, the Portuguese were shipping upward of eight hundred enslaved people per year from Arguin Island.

Portugal led the way in establishing an advanced system of trading of humans on an international scale. In the beginning of the slavery enterprise, Portugal relied exclusively on African leaders and traders for their captives, but when their demand for enslaved people to cultivate plantations along the coast of Africa, in the Caribbean, and in Brazil increased, they mounted direct attacks on coastal African peoples in hopes of enslaving larger numbers on their own.

Early on, the Portuguese were no match for the African people they encountered, whose knowledge of maritime skills, the coastal terrain, and unique military tactics gave them a defensive advantage. One such scrimmage took place in 1444, when Portugal attacked the Wolof Empire in what is now Senegal to kidnap and enslave its people for their growing labor needs. But the Portuguese, underestimating Senegal's tactical skills and military might, failed in their attack.

Realizing that their only means of acquiring African slave labor was through their existing relationships with local African leaders and traders, they reestablished those arrangements to guarantee the continuous supply of slaves. But over time they changed their tactics for acquiring Africans for slave labor once again. Eventually the Portuguese returned with better armor and weapons, which enabled them to subdue the West and Central African peoples who had been supplying them with captives. Now the Portuguese were able to find and seize their own slaves, giving them a monopoly in the slave trade for years to come.

PORTUGAL SET ITS SIGHTS ON THE PEOPLES OF WEST AFRICA

The agrarian, or farming, lifestyles of West African people made them the most appealing and valuable slaves. Additionally, they were sedentary farmers—meaning they grew their food in the same nearby location every year, which made them easy to capture when they least suspected it. Their knowledge of farming and sophisticated agriculture in some areas would be essential to the growth and development of the colonies and then the United States for years to come.

As Europeans developed more advanced weapons, such as cannons and pistols, they set their sights on nomadic African ethnic groups that moved from place to place in search of food.

As mentioned earlier, some African chiefs and other tribal leaders would trade captured enemies to European slave traders. These insiders used their knowledge of the regional geography and local villages to ensnare unwitting African men, women, and children for the purpose of supplying Europeans with a steady stream of captives.

Why would Africans help European slavers and African chiefs kidnap people from other African tribal groups? Well, for starters, they saw slave trading as a strategy to amass wealth and, more important, to wield greater power over rival tribal groups.

In Africa, many prisoners of war from other regional ethnic groups lived among their captors, working, starting families, and even building homes in some instances, unless the warring factions struck a peace deal or formed a mutually beneficial alliance. Over time, some of these captives could earn their freedom. Some married members within the ruling kingdom became members of new tribal groups and, eventually, established new lives, far away from those they once knew.

But how rival African tribes treated their captured enemies and how the European slave traders treated the people they captured and took far away from their homeland were as different as night and day.

STOLEN FROM HOME, THEN HIDDEN IN PLAIN SIGHT

Africans who were captured and then sold to Europeans found themselves shackled together with strangers, bound for a strange land. Their journey as captives was brutal and inhumane from the very start. They were forced to walk hundreds of miles from the interior to the West African coast in a coffle—a line of enslaved people chained or tied together—not knowing where they were headed, or when or if they would ever see their families again. By the time they arrived at the coast, they were starving, dehydrated, and exhausted from the arduous and horrific trek that had taken them so far from home, from everything they knew and everyone they loved.

As news of the disappearance and capture of local men, women, and even children spread, parents and community elders rallied to keep loved ones safe, but they were no match for slave traffickers. White people devised cruel restraints to subdue and punish captive Africans. Forged out of iron, these shackles, manacles, and ghoulish face masks limited slaves' movement and their ability to turn completely around to see where they had come from, preventing captives from determining where they were being taken on the coast in relation to their villages.

Children wore shackles as well. In some cases, a mother would be shackled with her children. Some slave shackles even included basic identifiers of the captives, such as "Negro woman" or "Negro child."

The make and style of slave shackles, manacles, and face masks varied in their degree of restraint, but one thing is for sure: they were effective torture devices that made it nearly impossible for captive enslaved people to escape the snares of their white captors.

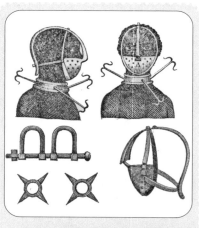

Experiencing this level of inhumanity, many fell into a great depression and could not be consoled by the

An iron mask, collar, leg shackles, and spurs used to restrain captured Africans.

other pitiful strangers they were fated to live with during their collective nightmare. Many tried to resist their iron chains, but to no avail. Their will to be free of their shackles and return to their families was overpowered by the iron restraints. Some did escape, only to be lost in the dense forests so far from home. Other attempts were thwarted, ending in recapture or death at the hands of the captors. A great many died along the way.

Once at the coast, they suffered even greater indignities as they were showcased before strange white men who poked, prodded, and inspected their naked bodies to determine their strength and value as slaves.

At West African coastal forts built by the Dutch, such as Cape Coast, Gorée Island, Bunce Island, and Elmina, captured Africans would spend up to *three months* imprisoned in dark, damp dungeons chained together with people they didn't know, and with little to no sunlight. Ghana's Cape Coast Castle was a chamber of horrors for over fifteen hundred captive African men, women, and children at a time. Captive men could number a thousand, with women routinely accounting for the remaining five hundred.

Captive Africans were forced to eat—if you can count the meager food they were given, which consisted of grains and palm oil—and relieve themselves in the same place where they slept and spent their days and nights. Those captives who tried to choose starvation rather than eat the unsavory provisions were force-fed.

The holding areas had very little ventilation, so the captives inhaled the stench of human waste, vomit, and the rotting flesh of those who died alongside them. The slave traffickers didn't even give them the dignity of bathing. They lay trapped in filth, hungry, thirsty, frightened, bewildered, and defenseless against enemies they didn't know they had. As terrible as all this was, they didn't realize that their nightmare was going to get far worse as time went along.

Captured Africans spent their days and nights in the slave castle dungeons and were allowed to come outside in the courtyards for only a few minutes of exercise each day. They suffered other terrors as well when their fellow captives experienced depression, fear, and anguish from their desperate plight, or when the sick among them died and they were trapped in the dark with infected bodies. Some rebelled, but to no avail. The slave castles were fortified inside and out, against both enemy attack and attempts to escape from within.

Certainly they longed to break free and make their way back to their villages and their families.

Surely they hoped that the doors of the dungeon and the castle would be flung open so that they could step into the light of a new day and escape their nightmarish conditions, as if awakening from a terrible dream.

THE DOOR OF NO RETURN

But when the castle door finally opened, it was like nothing they had dreamed about. It sealed their uncertain fates on the other side of the Atlantic Ocean, and for most it would never bring them any closer to the loved ones and the way of life they were forced to leave behind.

It was the Door of No Return.

Throughout the transatlantic slave trade, millions of Africans would be forced through doors of no return at forts along West African shorelines. It would

President Barack Obama and First Lady Michelle Obama looked out the "Door of No Return" during their tour of the Maison des Esclaves Museum on Gorée Island, Senegal, in 2013.

be the last glimpse of their native land. Today, forts like Elmina in Ghana and Senegal's "House of Slaves" on Gorée Island still remain as reminders of the terrible things that took place there.

THE MAAFA

Maafa is a Swahili term for "terrible occurrence" or "great disaster" and refers to the millions of captured African men, women, and children who perished during the Middle Passage—the forced journey from the west coast of Africa to shores of the Americas. Indeed, what the African people experienced once they arrived at their destination was compounded by the inhumane conditions of the journey itself. As in the castles, they were shackled to one another amid filth, death, vomit, and other bodily waste.

Slavers chained them together by their ankles, wrists, and necks. Men, women, and children were separated by sex and forced to sit or lie down, packed tightly into the bellies of massive ships without space to move about freely or even relieve themselves in private. Many of them suffered from motion sickness and regurgitated what little food they were given right there in the cramped human cargo space. Others became sick and infected those around them. It was virtually impossible to escape the stench or the sight of human waste since the enslaved Africans were packed so tightly into the cargo hold—a space designed to carry goods and supplies, not human beings.

After many jumped overboard to their deaths, their captors outfitted the massive slave vessels with netting to keep captives from plunging into the sea.

The captives were also brutally flogged, beaten into submission, and branded with the commercial seal of their captors. As horrific and heart-wrenching as this treatment was, it was nothing compared to the life in bondage they faced when they arrived in their new home—America.

THE NIGHTMARE THAT AWAITED THEM ON THE OTHER SIDE OF THE ATLANTIC OCEAN

Nearly 40 percent of the enslaved Africans who ended up in the United States and the West Indies disembarked from slave ships on the shores of Sullivan's Island, a barrier island just across the Cooper River and near Charleston, South Carolina. Charleston was a thriving port city made rich off slave labor used to cultivate rice, indigo, and cotton.

Those stolen Africans who survived the treacherous voyage were forced to quarantine aboard the disease-infested vessels or were moved to "pest houses"—dwellings used to house those afflicted with communicable diseases such as the plague—on the island, where they were isolated for weeks at a time to ensure they could not infect local residents and prospective buyers with any of the contagious diseases that had already claimed so many of their fellow captives.

The time they spent in quarantine was similar to their imprisonment in the slave castles, but it became much worse when they realized they had been transported to a foreign place so very far from home. The anguish they experienced led to deepened depression and despondency; not only were they separated from their families and loved ones, but now they had no idea which way led to home, *if* they ever had the chance to return.

But life was about to get even worse. Once they were released from quarantine, they were forced to march shackled and naked through the streets of Charleston for everyone to see. Men, women, and children were stripped of their meager clothing so that interested buyers could inspect them. It was a humiliating experience.

White men and women poked and prodded their bodies, peered into their mouths, and pulled on their limbs and genitals to satisfy their curiosity about the captives' abilities to do manual labor or, in the case of women and girls, produce offspring.

Some white men also had more insidious plans for the unsuspecting African women and girls. Once they had "purchased" them, many slave owners physically and emotionally abused the enslaved women and girls they owned. Many of them impregnated enslaved women in the same houses where their wives slept.

Of course, the slave owners' behavior angered their wives. But instead of taking their anger out on their husbands, white women directed their wrath at the helpless enslaved women, who had no rights and no one to defend them from the predatory power slave owners held over them. Like their male counterparts, white women could inflict cruel torture on enslaved women without recourse. They saw enslaved people simply as property they could handle however they wished.

Sarah Baartman, the "Venus Hottentot"

White people believed and promoted racist propaganda that explorers and prominent leaders wrote to document their first encounters with Black people in Africa. The explorers' travel logs and diaries are riddled with pornographic descriptions of African men and women they saw during their travels. Many included exaggerated details about their noses, lips, and hair, and many others wrote in great detail about their genitals and posteriors.

Take for example, the case of Sarah Baartman, also known as the "Venus Hottentot." Baartman was a Black woman from South Africa whose body was studied by French doctors and scientists and put on display for European people's entertainment during the 1800s. The term "Hottentot" was a derogatory

This print exaggerates Sarah Baartman's features and places a cupid on her body saying "Take care of your hearts."

slur Europeans used to refer to Baartman's tribe, the Khoikhoi, and to Black people generally.

Baartman astounded Europeans because she was afflicted with steatopygia, which basically means she had big buttocks. The illiterate Black woman, who was on her own after losing both her parents when she was very young, fell victim to a scheming con man who promised her steady work in his shows in England. In reality, the man had duped her into signing a contract to perform as a "freak" in his traveling entertainment shows.

Baartman didn't perform at all. Instead, dressed in tight clothing that accentuated her rear end, the poor woman suffered the gawking of inquiring minds. If that wasn't humiliating enough, rich white people could pay for private viewings during which they could physically inspect her body.

Sarah Baartman was objectified by white people for most of her life. They didn't see her as a person; they saw her as a freak of nature, and she piqued their curiosity about African people. For many, seeing her was enough to confirm the racist propaganda that flourished throughout the eighteenth century just as the international slave trade was booming.

There were people who tried to help the vulnerable young woman. In fact, abolitionists and other humanitarians took up her cause, but to no avail. In 1815, she died at the age of twenty-six. Even in death she continued to be objectified: a Paris museum kept Baartman's brain, skeletal remains, and organs on display until 1974.

Her experiences of exploitation and objectification are reflective of what enslaved women and girls in the United States experienced on the auction block, in the plantation Big House, and in the fields at the hands of white men.

• • •

SLAVERY WAS BIG BUSINESS

The transatlantic slave trade made many Europeans rich. The slave-trading nations included France, Britain, Spain, the Netherlands, and Portugal. In the beginning, Portugal led the pack. Portuguese slavers ultimately captured and enslaved nearly 4 million Africans, taking the lion's share of the captured to Brazil, which was a receiving station for over 3 million enslaved

Africans. But the British were not too far behind, transporting 3 million kidnapped Africans to North America and the Caribbean to provide labor for the growing colonies. British slave owners, both the rich and those of more modest means, used enslaved people to amass wealth for their business ventures abroad.

THE DUTCH WEST INDIA COMPANY QUICKLY OUTPACED PORTUGAL IN THE SLAVERY BUSINESS

One of the most profitable sixteenth- and seventeenth-century trading companies was the Dutch West India Company, established by the Netherlands. Also known as the West India Company, the international company had one primary goal: to quash the military and economic might of its competitors, Spain and Portugal. To do this, the Dutch had to beat both nations in the race to colonize new lands by setting up trading posts on the west coast of Africa and in Brazil, in the Caribbean, and alongside the Hudson River in what today is New York City.

Eventually, the company held a monopoly on the world's trading routes. For the better part of two centuries the Dutch West India Company led the trade of enslaved Africans throughout the world. However, competition in the lucrative industry was fierce, and as a result the Dutch West India Company also fought many battles to maintain its monopoly and protect the financial interests of the Netherlands. The Dutch didn't profit just from the sale of slaves, however. They used them to work in the Dutch colonies in the Caribbean, such as Curaçao, and settlements such as Dutch Guiana, known today as Suriname and Guyana, on the South American mainland.

THE DUTCH ESTABLISH NEW AMSTERDAM

The Dutch used both free and enslaved Africans along with German and English workers when they planted their flag and established New Amsterdam, on the island the Indigenous inhabitants, Lenape, called Manhatta—Manhattan, as it is known as today.

At first it looked like the Dutch and the Lenape might live together peacefully, sharing the land and trading goods like beads, guns, and wool. The Dutch are even said to have "purchased" Manhatta from the Lenape. However, the Lenape didn't have a concept for owning land. Instead, they thought they were

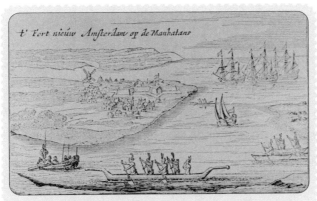

A 1651 illustration of New Amsterdam.

merely selling the Dutch the right to use their land. But that relationship quickly went bad when the Dutch built a huge wall to prevent Lenape access to land their ancestors had settled on over six thousand years before. Tensions between the Dutch and the Lenape went from bad to worse as the Dutch encroached upon more of their land and even tried to tax them. The bad blood between the two groups erupted into a full-blown battle known as Kieft's War, in which many on both sides lost their lives.

DUTCH NEW AMSTERDAM BECAME NEW YORK WITH SLAVE LABOR

In 1644, New Amsterdam was taken from the Dutch by British opponents, who changed its name to New York, after the Duke of York.

Seventeenth-century New York was nothing like today's bustling metropolis. The city that it became was made possible by a diverse labor force of Europeans of different backgrounds, along with free and enslaved Africans, who not only built it out of wilderness but also provided support for the British colonists' way of life. Enslaved Africans cut the timber, cleared and cultivated the land through farming, and built the houses and roads that would provide infrastructure. They were also forced to fight to protect the colony when necessary.

Just a century later, enslaved Africans and African Americans made up one-fifth of New York's population. New York played a mammoth role in the shipping and trade of textiles, food, and cotton, businesses made possible by booming slave labor in the South.

LET'S THINK ABOUT THIS:

1. Why were European slave traders successful in capturing and enslaving so many African people?

2. Did you know that slavery still exists today? Why do you think there isn't an international outcry about it?

3. The author William Faulkner wrote, "The past is never dead. It isn't even past." How can this quote help us understand how the legacy of slavery continues to shape American society today?

CHAPTER 2

NORTH AMERICA AT THE TIME OF THE COLONISTS' ARRIVAL

I f we are going to tell the truth about slavery in the United States, we have to go way back in time and reexamine a lot of the "truths" we have been taught about this nation. Sometimes this can be uncomfortable, but it can help us find answers to questions about our collective history as Americans. You might have already been wondering about some ideas or events that don't logically fit the rest of the historical puzzle we're putting together.

Let's take the "discovery of America," for example. How is it possible that the Italian explorer Amerigo Vespucci "discovered" a "new world" when it already had people living in it? Years after Christopher

Columbus's 1492 "discovery," Vespucci realized, during one of his expeditions, that South and North America were not parts of Asia, as Columbus had assumed. What he "discovered" was that they were two separate and unique landmasses. And this is why the names of both continents are attributed to him.

However, the long-held "truth" that the continents explored by Vespucci had not been "discovered" by anyone else doesn't accurately reflect what really happened when Europeans arrived in a new land and encountered its inhabitants. But that's how colonization works: You place yourself at the center of the narrative and act as if you have the right to conquer, own, displace, and subdue any and all people who stand in the way of what you believe to be your destiny or God-inspired mission. Understanding colonization is an important step toward examining and accepting the truth about slavery and the making of the United States.

THE COLONISTS STOLE FROM THE INDIGENOUS PEOPLE THEY MET AND THEN TRIED TO ENSLAVE THEM

When, about a hundred years after Vespucci, British colonists first arrived in North America, their mission was simple: settle down, seize the bountiful riches for the Crown, and secure the land. They were outnumbered by the Indigenous people they encountered, and they required the assistance of the very people they would go on to subdue and all but annihilate. With food scarce after weeks, sometimes months, of travel, and shelter nonexistent, they needed the help of the Native people for survival.

Some of the Indigenous communities the British encountered upon arrival were the Yamasee, Powhatan, and Wampanoag. At first the colonists and the Indigenous people had mutually beneficial arrangements; each group bartered with the other for the goods they wanted and needed. But that goodwill didn't last, and eventually the two groups became fierce rivals, who in some instances fought to the death over land. When it was all over, thousands of Indigenous people had lost their lives in battle or through exposure to deadly diseases such as smallpox, which the colonists brought with them and to which the Indigenous people had no immunity.

Yet once they had defeated the Indigenous nations and possessed their vast lands, the colonists realized that they didn't know the first thing about farming and agriculture in this new place. They also realized that if they were going to survive and thrive in the world they dreamed of building, they would need the help of a lot of people. So they tried to force the Indigenous people into slavery.

Enslaving the Indigenous people proved difficult. Because they knew the land well, they were hard to capture. And those who were captured frequently escaped, aided by their nearby tribal kinsmen. Some captured Indigenous people did not escape, but they outright rejected life as enslaved people by refusing to do the work they were ordered to do. Even more Indigenous people would suffer when Europeans introduced them to alcohol.

When the colonists' attempts to enslave the Indigenous people failed, they moved on to the indentured servitude of poor people from Europe, most of whom were white, to support their lifestyles in the Americas.

● ● ●

Indentured Servants

While indentured servants endured harsh working conditions, poor living conditions, and sometimes violent punishment, their experiences were different from those of slaves. First, many willingly signed contracts agreeing to work for a specified amount of time in exchange for passage from Europe to the colonies plus room and board as their sole wages. At the end of those contracts, most were freed from their commitments. In some cases servants were forced into indenture out of desperation, or they were forced by family members as a way to settle debts. Even though many indentured servants suffered abuse, they did have rights, unlike slaves, who did not.

The first indentured servants arrived shortly after the establishment of Jamestown in 1607. The settlers had a lot of land to develop and needed cheap labor to help with the daunting task of making the new and uncharted land their home. To do this, they recruited poor and desperate men and women in Europe who had very little to lose, transporting them to work in North America for a specified period of time. For their part, indentured servants were given room, food, and *freedom dues*—payment at the end of their contract, including a parcel of land on which to settle down and build a home.

Indentured servants worked hard under oppressive conditions. They were punished harshly for infractions such as trying to run away. Female indentured servants were punished if they became pregnant, because they would be incapable of carrying out the terms of their work contracts if they had to care for a child. They could be flogged or jailed for crimes or anything deemed bad behavior.

But even though there were a lot of poor white people who were desperate enough to sign on to indentured servitude, there weren't enough of them for the settlers. And that's when the colonists turned to buying and enslaving African people.

• • •

BEFORE SLAVERY, COLONISTS DID SOME OF THE SAME WORK THEY WOULD FORCE ENSLAVED PEOPLE TO DO FOR FREE

Many white people themselves did the arduous work that enslaved Africans were later brought in to do. During the period between the establishment of Jamestown in 1607 and the arrival of the first enslaved Africans twelve years later, white men and women—sometimes with the assistance of indentured servants—did their own farming in the Northern, Southern, and middle colonies. But it was arduous, backbreaking work, and they eventually turned to slave labor to build their homes and communities in the New World. And over time their use of slave labor not only helped to build the American colonies but also helped many colonists amass personal wealth. So greed, not need, gave birth to chattel slavery in America.

THE UNFORTUNATE FATE OF JOHN PUNCH

The first Black man to be enslaved for life in the North American colonies was John Punch, who was first an indentured servant in the colony of Virginia. Like white indentured servants, Punch was contracted to work for a man named Hugh Gwyn for a specific number of years. However, during his time working for Gwyn, Punch was treated more like a slave. He wasn't the only one who felt this way. Along with a Dutchman named Victor and a Scot named James Gregory, two of his white counterparts, Punch fled his indentured post in 1640. When the crew were apprehended, Victor and James Gregory were sentenced to an additional year of labor for their crimes. Punch, however, was sentenced to enslavement for the rest of his life.

Punch's case marked the beginning of a systematic practice of sentencing Black people to much harsher punishment for the same crimes committed by white people. More important, it set the stage for future laws that would legalize slavery based on race and ensure that enslaved Black people and their offspring had no rights for generations to come.

SLAVERY WASN'T ALWAYS SIMPLY BLACK AND WHITE

Just as some Africans played central roles in the trafficking and sale of African people to European slave traders, some Black people in America bought and owned enslaved people for profit. While the numbers of Black slaveholders are minuscule compared to white slaveholders, they did exist.

In some instances, formerly enslaved and freeborn Black people alike enslaved people who looked just like them or had a shared story of bondage. They willingly participated in the systemic oppression of other Black people to support their livelihood in farming and other trades.

In fact, one of the earliest documented court cases involving slavery was brought by John Casor, an indentured Black man, who appealed to the court because Anthony Johnson, a free Black man, refused to set him free after his indentured service was complete.

The cruel irony of this story is that Johnson himself had been forced into indentured servitude in Virginia in 1621 during the early days of colonial life. Throughout his bondage, Johnson labored arduously on tobacco plantations and knew firsthand the trials of the indentured. Like most indentured servants of the time, Johnson was eventually given his freedom and was able to make a life for himself after his service contract was fulfilled.

Some might consider Johnson a success story. By 1651, Johnson, who had arrived as an indentured African in 1621, now owned five servants of his own, including John Casor, who sued him for his freedom because he had fulfilled the terms of his service contract. Unfortunately for Casor, the Virginia court sided with Johnson, who claimed that Casor's contract was indenture for life and not for any set term of

The handwritten ruling sentencing John Casor to a life of enslavement.

years, as Casor argued in his lawsuit. The court ruled in Johnson's favor and demanded that "John Casor Negro forthwith returne unto the service of his said master Anthony Johnson."

In the end, Casor was sentenced to a life of enslavement, even though he contended that he had been an indentured servant and not a slave.

To a much lesser degree, indentured servitude of poor white people continued in some places throughout slavery. Eventually, chattel slavery replaced the indentured servitude of Black people, making them, like John Casor, enslaved for life.

LET'S THINK ABOUT THIS:

1. Why did the colonists treat the Indigenous people they encountered the way they did?

2. Are there any similarities between the way early European explorers treated the African people they encountered and the way the colonists treated the Indigenous people they encountered or the enslaved Africans they used for free labor?

3. In the North American colonies, why did slavery become more appealing than indentured servitude, which also guaranteed the colonists a steady supply of workers who didn't have to be paid for their service?

4. What does the fact that some Black people in the British colonies were themselves slave owners say about the perceived value of Black life?

CHAPTER 3

AMERICAN LAWS MADE SLAVERY LEGAL

lave codes were laws that outlined every aspect of slavery and authorized white people's power over slaves and, in most cases, free Black people as well. Very early on, the colonists pondered what to do about the growing slave enterprise happening right before their eyes. The 1619 arrival of the first captured Africans in Jamestown occurred even before they had put in place legal measures to establish slavery.

In 1641, Massachusetts became the first state to codify slavery, followed by Connecticut in 1650. The other colonies, however, were not too far behind.

IMPORTANT DATES REGARDING SLAVERY IN
The AMERICAN COLONIES

DELAWARE

Transported from the West Indies in 1639, a man named Anthony is the first enslaved African in the colony.

MASSACHUSETTS

The first enslaved people arrive in the 1630s, and slavery is codified in 1641. It's the first colony to legalize slavery.

NEW YORK

Dutch colonists transport the first enslaved people to New Amsterdam in 1626; once it becomes New York under British rule, slavery is institutionalized in 1664.

CONNECTICUT

Enslaved people arrive in the 1630s, but slavery isn't legalized until 1650. By the time of the American Revolution, Connecticut has more enslaved people than any of the other New England colonies.

NEW HAMPSHIRE

In 1645, slave merchants bring a captured African from Guinea, making him the first enslaved person in the colony.

RHODE ISLAND

Colonists first enslave the Indigenous Pequot, Narragansett, and Wampanoag after a war with the Pequot in 1637. In 1696, the slave ship Seaflower arrives carrying forty-seven captive Africans; fourteen are sold to residents of Newport, Rhode Island.

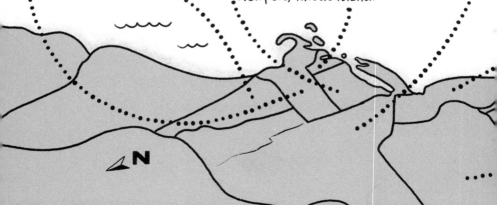

CAROLINA

The first enslaved Africans are transported in 1526 into what is now South Carolina. The first slave codes are established in 1690. In the late 1600s and early 1700s, the first enslaved people were brought to what will become North Carolina; North Carolina's first slave code was enacted in 1715, when it split from South Carolina.

VIRGINIA

The first enslaved people arrive in 1619, and slavery is codified in 1661. As of 1682, any Black person brought to Virginia as a "servant" is deemed enslaved for life.

NEW JERSEY

Slavery is established in the Dutch colony of New Netherlands in the mid-1600s. When it becomes a British colony, financial incentives for slave owners are written into the first constitution in 1654–55.

MARYLAND

In 1642, thirteen Africans arrive in Saint Mary's, located in southern Maryland. In 1664, slavery is codified.

PENNSYLVANIA

The ship Isabella delivers 150 enslaved Africans to the port of Philadelphia in 1684.

GEORGIA

Georgia was the last colony added and the farthest south. Slavery was banned for its first nineteen years as a colony, but the ban was lifted after years of pressure in 1751.

A LEGAL SYSTEM FUELED BY A CULTURE OF WHITE SUPREMACY

Early colonial laws, followed by slave codes, gave white people the right to treat enslaved people like private property and nothing more. Legal dominion over enslaved people was rooted in a belief in whites' superiority over Black people.

This false thinking would lead to the development of some of the United States' most inhumane state and national laws. These racist laws laid the ground-work for ever more oppressive legislation that would make discrimination against Black people legal for over two hundred years.

Take, for example, Article 35 of Louisiana's 1825 Civil Code, which states, "A slave is one who is in the power of a master *to whom he belongs.* The master may *sell him, dispose of his person,* his industry and his labor: he can do nothing, *possess nothing, nor acquire* any thing, but what must belong to his master" [italics added].

In other words, a slave's life was not his or her own, but that of the master.

Can you even imagine thinking of a human being the way you think of your pet? Well, slave codes basi-cally made it legal and easy for white people to think of enslaved people in the same way they thought of their livestock or their carriages—*things* they owned and used to make their work easier, their businesses more profitable, and their lives more comfortable and enjoyable.

A Kentucky slave code described enslaved people as real estate that could be passed down to a slave owner's heirs. Some slave codes, such as a 1798 Maryland act, considered enslaved people personal property: "such as slaves, working beasts, animals of any kind, stock, furniture, plate, books, and so forth."

And a 1740 South Carolina act outlined the fate of slaves, their children, and any children they might have in the future:

All their issue and their offspring, born or to be born, shall be, and are hereby declared to be, and remain FOREVER HEREAFTER absolute slaves, and shall follow the condition of the mother and shall be deemed, held, taken reputed, and adjudged in the law to be chattels personal in the hands of their owners and possessors, and their executors, and administrators, and assigns to all intents, constructions, and purposes whatsoever.

That means that slaves, their children, *and* their children's children would be enslaved forever.

This particular law was established to guarantee

the inability of the enslaved to ever gain freedom and to ensure absolute control over them by limiting their ability to gather among themselves, other than for work purposes, which white people worried would lead to rebellion.

Some of the many slave codes gave white people the power to

- *have complete control over enslaved people;*
- *dictate the type of work enslaved people did, including how long they worked and the conditions under which they worked;*
- *feed and clothe enslaved people in the manner they saw fit;*
- *forbid the education and religious training of enslaved people; and*
- *imprison any enslaved person who refused to heed a master's command.*

Slave codes also outlined what enslaved people couldn't do under the law, such as

- *own property;*
- *travel and move about freely;*
- *control any wages they earned on behalf of white people;*

- *marry white people;*
- *gather to worship;*
- *socialize in small groups among one another;*
- *strike a white person in self-defense; and*
- *use the law to sue for freedom or personal injury at the hands of white people.*

Colonial, and later state, slave codes, followed by federal laws, governed the institution of slavery and the lives of enslaved people and their descendants, making it virtually impossible for Black people, enslaved or free, to escape white tyranny.

WHITE PEOPLE USED THEIR BELIEF IN THEIR OWN SUPREMACY TO JUSTIFY SLAVERY

Many white people actually believed that slavery was good for the captured Africans and the African Americans who were born into slavery. Slave owners and pro-slavery advocates believed that Black people were inferior and that they needed white people to control them, regulate their movement, determine how they lived, and decide what they ate and drank. In this way slavery treated Black people like infants, reducing them to childlike individuals who needed supervision and punishment by white people to teach them their place in the world. White people called adult men "boy" and called women "gal" to reinforce their dominance.

In reality, whites' violent and systemic control of enslaved people only served *their* best interests. Slave owners, overseers, slave drivers, slave catchers, and plantation mistresses alike were guilty of torturing slaves. Torture was completely legal, unless a person was guilty of harming or killing another man's slave. In that case the crime was against the slave owner, and not against the actual victim of the offense, the slave.

White people beat, branded, hanged, burned, and even skinned enslaved people alive. When enslaved people ran away, their owners sent bloodthirsty hounds to savage them limb from limb. They also made them torture one another. An overseer might make a husband whip his wife for an infraction, tearing open the flesh on her back. Pregnant women were not spared either. In some instances, a woman would be made to lie naked, her pregnant belly forced into a hole in the ground and her back exposed to the violent lash.

If we want reminders of how badly enslaved people were treated, we need look no further than a Civil War–era photograph of a runaway enslaved man named Gordon. Harriet Tubman, the most famous Underground

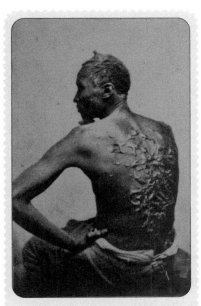

Gordon, a formerly enslaved man who escaped, showed his scarred back at a medical examination in 1863.

Railroad conductor (we will learn about her later), helped him escape captivity. Like others who ran away during the Civil War, Gordon found safety and refuge at a Union Army camp along the Mississippi River. There, in 1863, Gordon's battered and scarred back was photographed by William D. McPherson and J. Oliver. These two photographers captured many images of former slaves, but none were more moving than the image of Gordon, known as "The Scourged Back."

The cat-o'-nine-tails was a particularly insidious weapon. Exceptionally cruel plantation overseers and slave drivers used this whip, made of leather and rope. It typically had nine "tails," each knotted at the end, to inflict several harsh wounds with each lash of the whip. The "cat" was first used aboard the slave ships that brought kidnapped Africans to parts throughout the Americas. In North America, it was the weapon of choice to inflict fear, punish slaves, and keep them in line.

White people developed other devices to torture enslaved people as punishment, too. Some devices stretched slaves' bodies so that the limbs became disjointed. Others, like the neck collar, limited their ability to move or see what was happening around them, and some covered the whole face, exposing only the eyes, with no opening to speak or eat through.

Notoriously cruel overseers, drivers, and slave owners were feared by both enslaved people under their watch and those who only knew of their reputations. One of the most sinister slave owners was a woman in New Orleans. In the 1830s, Madame Delphine LaLaurie shocked even other white slave owners with her diabolical deeds. Her enslaved people were always going "missing," and people regularly heard screams and cries from her mansion. Rumors circulated among her neighbors and other residents about the unthinkable punishments she inflicted upon her slaves, but no one could say for sure if the rumors were actually true or simply gossip.

That is, until one enslaved woman set a fire in the house, thinking she would rather die than continue to be tortured. When authorities arrived, the old

*The LaLaurie Mansion,
shown in 2022.*

woman was chained to a stove. She told her rescuers that she feared her mistress might send her to the attic of the house, because the enslaved people who went up there never returned.

The men went up to the attic, and what they found sickened and shocked them. LaLaurie had her very own torture chamber. Enslaved people were bound in metal contraptions, starved, and even forced to eat feces. Some were suspended by hooks in their skin. They were mutilated and burned. It was a living hell. Elsewhere on the property they found the graves of other enslaved people LaLaurie had tortured and killed.

In any other Southern state, LaLaurie's extremely cruel treatment of her enslaved people wouldn't have been considered criminal behavior. However, eighteenth-century Louisiana had a unique set of laws governing slavery known as the Code Noir, or Black Code, which gave enslaved people there some "rights" under the law. For example, enslaved people could marry whom they wanted—as long as it was another Black person—and their owners had to grant their baptism in the Catholic Church and allow them to attend mass on Sundays. It also prohibited severe punishment of enslaved people.

LaLaurie was ordered to pay fines for her criminal behavior. But before justice could be served, she fled New Orleans. When local residents learned about Madame LaLaurie's extreme cruelty, they stormed her home, destroying many of her belongings and doing great damage to the house as well.

WHITE PEOPLE CREATED LAWS TO KEEP ENSLAVED PEOPLE FROM LEARNING TO READ AND WRITE

During slavery, white people enacted many laws to keep Black people—both enslaved and free—from learning to read and write. White slaveholders recognized the power of literacy to transform people's lives and inspire them to dream and think for themselves. They certainly didn't want that for the people they held as slaves. They assumed that by keeping Black people illiterate, they could maintain power over them.

They assumed wrong! Even though the majority of enslaved Black people could not read or write, they could reason for themselves. Just as the Founding Fathers believed British rule over their lives and affairs in America was oppressive, enslaved people knew that their lifelong bondage and subjugation were wrong. This was especially true for those who remembered their lives in Africa, before captivity. But even those who were born into slavery and had never lived any other way understood the power of living as free people.

Learning to read and write English wasn't the easiest thing for captive Africans to do. The Africans who were brought to the United States came from largely oral traditions—in which history and folklore are learned and passed down by memory recitation, rather than written in books—so seeing white people reading and writing was strange for sure. But even without understanding what reading was, many enslaved Africans felt there was a power in books. In *The Classic Slave Narratives,* the collection by Henry Louis Gates Jr., formerly enslaved people such as Olaudah Equiano, Frederick Douglass, and Harriet Jacobs described the great lengths to which white people went to keep the enslaved populace illiterate, and the parallel insatiable desire of those they oppressed to learn to read and write.

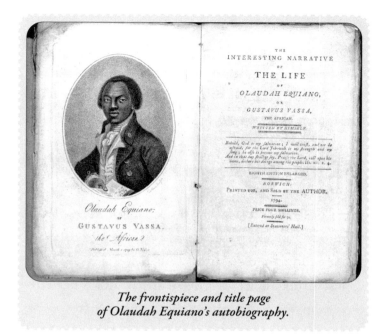

*The frontispiece and title page
of Olaudah Equiano's autobiography.*

In *The Interesting Narrative of the Life of Olaudah Equiano or Gustavus Vassa, the African,* Olaudah Equiano describes the fascination he experiences when he sees his master and his old friend Dick reading:

I had often seen my master and Dick employed in reading; and I had a great curiosity to talk to the books, as I thought they did; and so to learn how all things had a beginning: for that purpose I have often taken up a book, and have talked to it, and then put my ears to it, when alone, in hopes it would answer me; and I have been very much concerned when I found it remained silent.

Despite his initial misconception about books, Equiano was a quick study, which helped him in a number of ways. As luck would have it, in 1765 his last owner, Robert King, promised to let Equiano buy his freedom for the sum of forty pounds, which is over 10,000 US dollars today. Equiano worked very hard to earn the money. King, like some other slave owners, allowed Equiano to earn money of his own when he was done working for his master. It was during his free time that Equiano became skilled at selling goods. Pretty soon he had earned forty-seven pounds, which he offered to King to cover his original asking price plus interest. Once he had purchased his freedom, Equiano went on to learn how to read and write. His autobiography, published in 1789, was widely read and highly influential.

Frederick Douglass, one of the most influential Black abolitionists, was born and raised on plantations in Maryland. Douglass's yearning for freedom was fueled by separation from his family, by the unimaginable physical violence he endured at the hands of his master and plantation overseer, and by his awareness of the injustices other enslaved people suffered—an awareness that he gained as a result of learning to read.

Douglass witnessed the measures white people took to keep enslaved people from learning to read and write, and their violent wrath at the mere suspicion that an enslaved person was interested in learning. As a youngster living on Hugh and Sophia Auld's plantation, he had the very good fortune of having a kind mistress who took an interest in teaching him to read and write. But when Hugh discovered their lessons, he demanded that Sophia stop teaching the boy. Hugh believed that education would lead to rebelliousness—a common belief among white people at that time.

Of course, young Douglass was disappointed that his lessons had come to an end, and he was also deeply saddened that his once gentle and compassionate mistress had suddenly turned cold, suspicious, and violent at the mere sight of the boy holding a book or a newspaper. But his dream of literacy wouldn't die. He had learned the alphabet—and soon he had a new plan for learning to read and write. In his 1845 autobiography, he explained:

> *The plan which I adopted, and the one by which I was most successful, was that of making friends of all the little white boys whom I met in the street. As*

many of these as I could, I converted into teachers. With their kindly aid, obtained at different times and in different places, I finally succeeded in learning to read. When I was sent of errands, I always took my book with me, and by going one part of my errand quickly, I found time to get a lesson before my return. I used also to carry bread with me, enough of which was always in the house, and to which I was always welcome; for I was much better off in this regard than many of the poor white children in our neighborhood. This bread I used to bestow upon the hungry little urchins, who, in return, would give me that more valuable bread of knowledge. I am strongly tempted to give the names of two or three of those little boys, as a testimonial of the gratitude and affection I bear them; but prudence forbids;—not that it would injure me, but it might embarrass them; for it is almost an unpardonable offence to teach slaves to read in this Christian country. It is enough to say of the dear little fellows, that they lived on Philpot Street, very near Durgin and Bailey's ship-yard. I used to talk this matter of slavery over with them. I would sometimes say to them, I wished I could be as free as they would be when they got to be men. "You will be free as soon as you are twenty-one, but I am a slave for life! Have

*not I as good a right to be free as you have?" These
words used to trouble them; they would express for
me the liveliest sympathy, and console me with the
hope that something would occur by which I might
be free.*

His stick-to-itiveness would pay off. Once armed
with the ability to read, write, and speak passionately
about the horrors of slavery, he became one of the
most persuasive orators of the nineteenth century. He
used his firsthand experiences coming of age as an
enslaved person to denounce the institution of slavery. His popularity and power of persuasion were
white slaveholders' greatest fears realized!

To keep enslaved people illiterate, white lawmakers
developed harsh punishments for any enslaved person
caught reading or learning to read. These included
violent acts such as the cutting off of fingers and
limbs. It was even a crime for white people—or Black
people who were literate—to teach free or enslaved
Black people to read and write. Those who found a
way to learn to read and write had to go to great pains
to keep their skills a secret.

Keeping enslaved people from reading was just
another way to indoctrinate them with the idea that
white supremacy ruled and Black lives didn't matter

other than to serve the plantation class, white elites, and even the lowliest of white people. As enslaved Africans and African Americans began to outnumber whites in certain communities, the threat of a Black majority that could read, write, and reason was a possibility that had to be fought at every turn.

But even with the legal barriers white people put in place to prevent enslaved and free Black people from learning to read and write, many—like Frederick Douglass—prevailed in their secret mission to become literate.

Once literate, enslaved and free Black people used the written word to demonstrate their—and, by extension, all Black people's—intellectual capabilities by becoming prolific and eloquent writers. For example, a young woman named Phillis Wheatley became one of the most beloved and highly acclaimed poets of the eighteenth century.

A portrait of Phillis Wheatley writing at her desk, which was used in the frontispiece of her first book of poems.

When she was a little girl of age seven or eight, Wheatley was stolen from her home in Senegambia and transported to Boston's docks, where she was purchased in 1761 by John Wheatley and his wife, Susanna, who wanted a domestic servant to support their household. Of course, little Phillis didn't speak any English. But she was a quick learner!

And there was more to the little girl. Sensing something remarkable in their house servant, the Wheatleys decided to teach her to read and write when she wasn't busy with her chores. With her new-found skills, their prize pupil began devouring books on the subjects of history, geography, and astronomy, along with the Bible, which made a lasting impact on Phillis's thinking and worldview.

In time, it became evident that Phillis was a gifted writer. John Wheatley had a thriving business as a tailor and moneylender. Early in his career he had served as a police officer, and the Wheatleys were a wealthy and influential family. Teaching enslaved people to read was illegal in Boston during those days, but John Wheatley's circle of prominent friends shielded the couple from trouble with the law.

At age thirteen, Phillis became a published writer when her poem "On Messrs Hussey and Coffin," about a narrowly avoided tragedy at sea, ran in the *Newport Mercury,* a Rhode Island newspaper. This was followed three years later by another poem, entitled "An Elegiac Poem, on the Death of That Celebrated Divine, and Eminent Servant of Jesus Christ, the Reverend and Learned George Whitefield," printed by the Boston publishers Ezekiel Russell and John Boyle.

Phillis quickly became an internationally recognized poet, and the Wheatleys supported her work and took her to meet dignitaries around the world, though she wouldn't be freed until the fall of 1773, not long before Susanna's death.

It is believed that Phillis wrote as many as 145 poems throughout her life. She did not devote a great deal of her writing to the subject of slavery, but when she did, she appealed to white Christians to recognize the humanity of enslaved people as cause for abolition:

> But how, presumptuous shall we hope to find
> Divine acceptance with th' Almighty mind—
> While yet (O deed ungenerous!) they disgrace
> And hold in bondage Afric's blameless race;
> Let virtue reign—And those accord our prayers
> Be victory our's, and generous freedom theirs.

Sadly, after her benefactors passed away, Phillis struggled to make a living during the tumultuous years of the Revolutionary War. She died in 1784, at just thirty-one years old. Nevertheless, Phillis Wheatley's talent, global reach, and critical acclaim are evidence of the great achievements thousands of enslaved people might have made had they been allowed to read and write.

CHRISTIANITY WAS USED TO VALIDATE SLAVERY, BUT ENSLAVED PEOPLE DIDN'T BUY IT

Keeping enslaved people illiterate worked hand in glove with attempts to strip the kidnapped Africans of their native languages, cultures, and religions. Since religion can affect people's everyday lives in profound ways, Christianity became one of the tools slave owners used to drill into enslaved people their lowly place in society. They did this by forcing the Africans and African Americans to attend church services that taught them a perverse version of Christianity.

The slave owners' version of Christianity was based upon select Bible verses that seem to condone slavery. It focused on passages from the books of

Ephesians and Colossians that include ideas like "servants, obey in all things your masters" to convince enslaved people that their subjugation was part of the natural order.

Some white slave owners and pro-slavery advocates believed that the enslavement of Black people was preordained in the Old Testament. The story, from Genesis 9:20–27, goes like this: After building the Ark and saving humanity, Noah gets drunk on wine one night, takes off his clothes, and falls asleep in his tent. His youngest son, Ham, sees him and runs to tell his older brothers, Japheth and Shem, who drape a garment over their shoulders, walk backward into the tent so that they won't see their father, and cover him with the garment. When Noah wakes up, he realizes that Ham has seen him naked and in a drunken stupor. Angry and ashamed, Noah curses Ham's son Canaan, saying he should be a servant to Japheth and Shem.

Pro-slavery white Christians argued that Ham's descendants were Black people, and that white people were the descendants of Japheth and Shem (even though the Bible says no such thing). They believed that God had given them a divine duty to oppress Black people. They used this belief to justify the inhumane treatment of slaves, as well as to create a legal system that viewed Black people as nothing more than "movable property."

White Christian slave owners also used the Bible to justify beating their slaves. They often quoted Ephesians 6:5–8 as divine justification for slaves' servitude to their masters and for inflicting fear and torture onto slaves:

> *Servants, be obedient to them that are your masters according to the flesh, with fear and trembling, in singleness of your heart, as unto Christ;*
>
> *Not with eye-service, as menpleasers; but as the servants of Christ, doing the will of God from the heart;*
>
> *With good will doing service, as to the Lord, and not to men:*
>
> *Knowing that whatsoever good thing any man doeth, the same shall he receive of the Lord, whether he be bond or free.*

White people erroneously believed that forcing enslaved people to listen to such biblical passages would help them accept their life of servitude. But in other passages, especially those about the Jews of the Old Testament, enslaved Africans and African Americans heard stories that not only were similar to the ones passed down to them from their ancestors but also had parallels to their lives in bondage. They saw themselves in the same plight as the Israelites who had been enslaved in Egypt, and upon hearing about the miraculous way the God of Israel had used Moses to part the Red Sea and deliver the Jews from the clutches of their Egyptian captors, enslaved people were encouraged that in this new world God would do the same for them.

When enslaved people and free Black people secretly learned to read and began to study the Bible for themselves, many embraced it as a beacon of hope for future liberation. Many of the most vocal and radical abolitionists used the Bible to argue for the end of slavery.

White people assumed that the enslaved Africans and African Americans had been totally stripped of their African pasts. They had not. In fact, they held on to memories of their native lands and passed them on to their children, families, and friends. Some of their spiritual traditions were blended with Christianity to create a unique way of worship that eventually formed the basis of the Black church in America.

Even today, if you ever attend a Black church, you might hear remnants of West African spiritual traditions such as the following:

- **Ring shout:** *a circular spiritual dance enslaved people did on plantations. This tradition originated with the juba, or African circle dance. Dancers sing and pray in a circular motion and get "happy" with the Holy Spirit.*

- **Hymn lining:** *a musical tradition in which a singer sings a line of a song and the congregants repeat it. Although this practice has English and Scottish roots, it is also rooted in the West African oral tradition of call-and-response, which allows participation by all members of the community.*

- **Percussive music:** *a musical tradition of drumming that enslaved Africans brought with them. Drums weren't just musical instruments; they were also important tools for communication, signaling danger, war, and celebratory times. During slavery, drums were used not only to entertain and uplift the spirits of enslaved people but also to alert them to trouble on the horizon or to signal time for uprising.*

- **Black sermonic tradition:** *the Black preaching style, rooted in West African oratory and storytelling. During slavery, plantation preachers like Nat Turner used their gifts of speech to inspire and organize fellow enslaved people in rebellion. Twentieth-century civil rights leaders such as Dr. Martin Luther King Jr. and Malcolm X embodied* *this stylized preaching to appeal to Black people, who were still fighting for their human and civil rights more than a hundred years after slavery ended.*

In the end, those stolen Africans who were brought to the British colonies and then to the United States as enslaved people and their descendants may have been forced to practice the religion of their white captors, but what they made of that religion has served them for several centuries and counting.

LET'S THINK ABOUT THIS:

1. Why did white people want to keep enslaved people illiterate?

2. Why did white people create slave codes when they already had power over the slaves?

3. How did the belief in white supremacy fuel white people's views both about enslaved people and about themselves?

CHAPTER 4

CREATING A NEW AMERICAN CULTURE

What must it have been like for the captive Africans who didn't understand the language of their captors or even the language of the other captives they encountered? Earlier, you learned that European slave catchers held Africans from different ethnic groups together in slave dungeons prior to the Middle Passage. There, frightened, confused, and depressed captives were isolated even further because they could not readily communicate with the other captives.

They could not understand the harsh commands that the slave catchers and the ship hands hurled at them, either. Although they would not have known what their captors were saying exactly, they could tell from the speakers' volume, intonation, gestures, and body language that their intentions were not good. Clearly, the white men meant them harm.

Once they were transported to their final destinations and forced to work as slaves, they faced further language barriers. The white slave owners, plantation overseers, and slave drivers they encountered spoke Spanish, Irish, French, and English. However, English was predominantly spoken among slavers in what would eventually become the United States, so enslaved people here were forced to learn it.

At first, a creole (mixed) language emerged combining the English that white people spoke and the different languages the enslaved Africans spoke. Enslaved people used the English words they learned along with words from their native tongues to communicate. Over time, as they learned more words from the English colonists, the enslaved people from different regions of Africa, and the Indigenous people they encountered and sometimes lived among, they created several unique dialects. For example, in the American colonies, Atlantic Creole (or Plantation Creole) emerged out of English and West African languages.

In the Low Country of South Carolina and Georgia, the Gullah Geechee dialect was spoken by enslaved people who were brought from what is now Sierra Leone. Gullah Geechee is still spoken in African American households throughout the sea islands of this region.

When enslaved people developed their own distinct dialect combining English and their native languages, *cultural syncretism* happened. This is when two or more cultures merge together to create a new cultural custom or tradition. Even though they were forced to learn English for survival, enslaved people used it in their own way.

This is what Lorenzo Dow Turner found in his research on Southern Black plantation language in the Georgia and South Carolina sea islands. Turner, who was born in 1890 and is recognized as America's first Black linguist, discovered over four thousand African words in use in Gullah Geechee communities in Georgia, South Carolina, and Florida—terms like *goober,* which means peanut, and *kuta* or *cooter,* which means turtle. These words give us proof of important African retentions enslaved people and their free descendants have been able to keep alive.

And there are many words regarded as standard American English that have African origins. For example, at Thanksgiving, your family probably eats turkey, stuffing, green beans, and yams or sweet potatoes. Well, yams are starchy root vegetables found in West Africa. They look similar to sweet potatoes, but yams have a tough brown exterior resembling tree bark, while sweet potatoes can be red or purple and have a sweet, smooth consistency. Yams and sweet potatoes are very distant relatives to each other (and distant from potatoes, too).

When African people encountered sweet potatoes, they probably thought they resembled the comforting food staple from their homeland, *nyami,* and started calling them yams. Today, you can find the word *yam* in grocery stores across the country to identify sweet potatoes.

The word *goober* derives from *nguba,* from the Bantu language Kimbundu spoken in Angola. Have you ever eaten Goobers candy while at a movie theater? Now you know where the name comes from!

And do you drink Coca-Cola? It takes its name partly from one of its most important ingredients, the kola nut, which comes from West Africa.

Enslaved Africans also added their own oratory flavor to English when they mastered it. This is most evident in their use of storytelling as entertainment, but also in the preaching styles of the enslaved people, who used what they were taught about Christianity through biblical passages they had heard, to inspire their fellow bondsmen and bondswomen.

Back in Africa, the spoken word was used to re-count one's family tree, to document important events such as the births and deaths of tribesmen, and to teach important life lessons using allegories and metaphors. When possible, enslaved people used English and creole in the same way.

• • •

Br'er Rabbit

Have you ever heard of the Br'er Rabbit stories? Br'er Rabbit, or Brer or Brother Rabbit, is a trick-ster character that enslaved people brought with them to the United States and other parts of the *African diaspora,* places throughout the world to which African people and their descendants moved either voluntarily through migration or forcibly during slav-ery. This includes Europe, the Americas, and any-where you find communities of Africans and people of African descent living, working, and express-ing their cultural traditions. Today this includes just about all points on the globe.

Br'er Rabbit is a clever, scrappy rabbit who

outwits the bigger and more dangerous animals he encounters. Trickster characters appear in many West African folktale traditions as a way for people to understand the natural world, explain universal human behavior, and teach listeners that strength and power have less to do with size and more to do with clever thinking and the consequences of one's actions. These stories served as entertainment for enslaved people, who spent the majority of their time working. They also provided them with hope, as they saw in Br'er Rabbit's capers the possibility of outwitting their captors. Br'er Rabbit is always able to dupe his foes in ways they'd never suspect!

An engraving of Br'er Fox and Br'er Rabbit talking to each other, 1892.

But Black people weren't the only ones who enjoyed the tales featuring

Br'er Rabbit, and even today you can find his influence on American literature and children's cartoons.

One white writer named Joel Chandler Harris borrowed heavily from the Br'er Rabbit stories he heard to create a character named Uncle Remus, a funny and clever man who narrated stories about other characters who were always getting into and out of mischief.

Harris had enjoyed listening to the Br'er Rabbit stories enslaved people told on the Turnwold Plantation, where he had learned the printing trade. There, working for the newspaper publisher and plantation owner Joseph Addison Turner, Harris began writing poems and comedic prose.

Harris turned what he learned from enslaved people on the Turnwold Plantation into a successful career writing Uncle Remus stories, while the enslaved people who inspired his timeless literary treasures received no compensation or recognition. Today we would call Harris's actions *cultural appropriation.*

Many people also believe that Bugs Bunny was inspired by the Br'er Rabbit stories. The popular Looney Tunes character is always getting into trouble but uses his cunning thinking to get him out of jams. Just like Br'er Rabbit!

TO BE ENSLAVED WAS TO ALWAYS BE HUNGRY

Being enslaved was hard, scary, and physically exhausting. Imagine getting up before daybreak to work on a cotton, rice, tobacco, or sugar plantation without pay and doing it with very little food in your belly! That's what enslaved people experienced day in and day out.

Enslaved people were given meager weekly rations with which to prepare their own meals; they had to stretch these short supplies to feed their entire families. In some places their diets consisted of meat, such as pork, and cornbread. Other, luckier slaves, might have corn, peas, beans, ham bone, and a few other vegetables boiled up in a soup or stew as part of their daily food rations. To feed everyone, the soups and stews would have to be stretched by adding water. Overall, the food that enslaved people received each day barely contained the nutritional value needed in a healthy diet, much less fuel for the type of backbreaking manual labor they did from sunup to sundown.

In many parts of West Africa, people sit on the ground and share communal meals, using their hands instead of eating utensils. In America, this tradition was carried over out of necessity. With so little food between them, enslaved people might eat from the same pot or the same plate so that everyone got a little. Many enslaved people suffered from ailments associated with malnutrition, like rickets, a disease that softens bones and leads to symptoms like bowlegs due to vitamin D deficiency.

Pregnant women who didn't get proper nutrition and were forced to work right up to their deliveries often gave birth to babies with extremely low birth weights. Many of these tiny babies died at birth or shortly thereafter. The babies who did make it to childhood were often frail and small for their age due to a lack of nutritious foods. It wasn't unusual for hungry children to gather around pots they found outside kitchens and other outdoor cooking areas to scrape the bottoms for any leftover morsels.

Those enslaved people who worked in the Big House—the house where slave owners and their families lived, primarily on large Southern plantations (and to a lesser degree on Northern ones too)—or had the job of cooking for the white owners had more opportunities to get better scraps and leftovers from the white families they served. But the penalty for being caught stealing food—even scraps that had been thrown away—could be physical punishment, including the chopping off of the enslaved person's hand.

Even with so little to eat, enslaved people made do—and then some. With the scraps they were given and with their memories of food and cooking in their homeland, they created an African American culinary tradition that has become a staple of many American tables: soul food.

When industrious enslaved people caught rabbits, possums, or squirrels, they used the cooking traditions of their past, such as boiling, frying, and stewing, to create culinary delights that soothed their physical and spiritual hunger at the same time.

On some plantations, slave owners provided enslaved people with small gardening plots to grow their own food during their free time. This practice helped slave owners reduce the amount of money they spent to feed their slaves, and it gave enslaved people the feeling of freedom and the ability to care for themselves and their families. Wherever possible, enslaved people incorporated food from their homelands into their diets. They were able to do this by bringing seeds with them when they were captured. Just like the enslaved people, the seeds survived and made their way through the treacherous journey of the Middle Passage. Because of the ingenuity of the captives, Americans today can enjoy foods that originated in Africa, like okra, watermelon, black-eyed peas, and certain peppers.

Enslaved people also made use of regional New World vegetables, herbs, and meat that reminded them of foods from back home, like leafy greens and, as noted earlier in this chapter, sweet potatoes.

SLAVERY'S INFLUENCE ON AMERICAN FOOD

If you've ever eaten fried chicken—or fried anything—you have enslaved cooks to thank. Cooking with heavy palm oil to make spicy meats and stews is customary in West Africa, but this staple ingredient was unavailable to them in North America. With no palm oil, they improvised by using lard—fat from pigs—to deep-fry foods like chicken and fish.

And have you had a one-pot meal like beans and rice, gumbo, or a meaty stew? If so, you have tasted for yourself the types of meals enslaved people prepared when and if they were lucky enough to have the ingredients they needed.

What about hoppin' John? This soul food delicacy was typically prepared and eaten along with collard greens and cornbread on New Year's Day to welcome good luck for the new year. The hearty peas and greens, cooked with fatty meat like salt pork, were symbols of good favor and fortune enslaved people hoped for. The wide green collard leaves resembled paper money, and the peas represented gold. Today you can find this traditional African American meal in homes and restaurants throughout the United States, and not just on New Year's Day.

Dishes like hoppin' John strengthened the bodies of tired enslaved people after they had completed backbreaking work in the fields, but they also nurtured their weary spirits by giving them a taste of food they remembered from their homeland.

A delicious plate of hoppin' John.

And enslaved people weren't the only ones to enjoy the culinary delights they cooked up over the hearths and small stoves they used for feeding their families. White slave owners benefited the most from the cultural fusion enslaved people incorporated into their cooking. They used their cultural cooking traditions to transform the meat and vegetation available to create delicious meals for the white families they served.

There were also enslaved people in the White House who prepared meals for presidents, diplomats, and other dignitaries. Even after slavery had ended, Black cooks were hired for the White House kitchen. Enslaved people routinely made Southern dishes for the private meals of presidents who were originally from the South.

For example, variations on cornbread were favorites of two of our most influential presidents. President George Washington, who was from Virginia, loved hoecakes, small griddle cakes made with cornmeal, milk, and flour topped with butter and honey. President Lincoln, who was born in Kentucky, loved them too, but he called them corn cakes. (Another name for this breakfast item is Johnny cakes.)

Researchers who study Southern foodways have identified African influences on Southern cuisine eaten by Black and white people alike. Southern foodways are the cultural, social, economic, and geographical traditions involved in the cultivation, production, preparation, and consumption of food in the American South. By investigating Southern foodways, we can actually identify and taste foods that enslaved people used for making nourishing and delicious dishes on their own. When we see the same or similar dishes in other parts of the country, we have evidence of their enduring influence on American culture.

ENSLAVED PEOPLE USED CULTURAL KNOWLEDGE TO HEAL THEMSELVES

Because enslaved people were almost always working or caring for the white people who owned them, they had very little time to tend to their own needs. This was especially problematic when they or their loved ones fell ill.

And transmission of disease was rampant. Because they were malnourished, overworked, and crowded together in squalid housing—often without being supplied with what they needed to wash their clothes or maintain basic sanitation—enslaved people were very susceptible to all types of germs.

Doctors were rarely called in to treat enslaved people who were sick or injured. This forced those who were enslaved to rely on themselves and one another for help. Luckily, some of them had knowledge of medicinal plants and could create herbal remedies to heal everything from childhood illnesses to colds and other ailments. Their homemade treatments were so effective that white people used some of them as well.

Black plantation midwives used their knowledge of childbirth and delivery to usher the babies of enslaved women into the cruel world of slavery that awaited them. They also used their knowledge of herbs to help expectant bondswomen during their pregnancies and afterward. In many cases, midwives saved the lives of mothers and their babies.

Life for pregnant enslaved women was extremely difficult. They were forced to work in the field doing backbreaking labor, or perform domestic work like cleaning, cooking, and washing clothes, at the same pace as other enslaved servants. They never had enough food to eat or enough time to fully rest. Overseers forced them to work until they went into labor. After delivery they had very little, if any, time to bond with their babies. Most went back to work a day or so after giving birth; others were reassigned to the Big

House to nurse the babies of plantation mistresses. Believe it or not, enslaved mothers on Southern plantations were routinely separated from their own newborn babies and, while lactating (producing milk), were forced to serve as *wet nurses* for white babies instead. The custom of using wet nurses was a cultural practice that wealthy plantation and slave owners brought with them from Europe. There, lower-class white women were paid to nurse the children of rich white women.

Plantation midwives delivered white babies too. Their skills were called upon when a white physician wasn't available, and their expertise led to the safe delivery of babies born breech—buttocks first—or in other life-threatening situations.

Even after slavery was over in this country, Black midwives continued to deliver babies in the rural South well into the twentieth century, because Black people weren't welcome at white hospitals and didn't have hospitals of their own. However, as millions of African Americans moved out of the South and headed north, west, and east in search of work and educational opportunities for their children during the Great Migration—the largest migration of Black Americans from one region of the United States to another, beginning around 1916—midwifery drastically declined. Modern life in the big cities included access to better doctors and hospitals.

In recent decades, Black midwifery has made a comeback among Black mothers, couples, and doctors who see value and wisdom in this important tradition of their foremothers. Just as American midwifery grows in popularity among expecting parents, Black midwives deliver babies to couples of diverse races in hospitals and private homes throughout the country.

SLAVE MASTERS ENTRUSTED ENSLAVED PEOPLE WITH RAISING THEIR CHILDREN

Did you know that during slavery, many white children were practically raised by people their families owned? Although whites believed Blacks were inferior, they still entrusted them with the personal care of their most precious treasures: their children.

Enslaved Black men and women played influential roles in the lives of white children up through adolescence. The enslaved people who cared for white children fed, bathed, and clothed them; nursed their wounds; and taught them right from wrong. The Black women, in particular, who raised white babies formed strong maternal bonds with them. These same white children, whom they loved and who loved them in return, would often inherit them as property when their parents died. In most instances, the bonds between enslaved people and the white children they had raised were not enough to break the strong hold of slavery.

Even after slavery had ended, many Black women in the North and the South could find only domestic work as maids and nannies for white families. But Black men also found work as butlers and caretakers for white children as well. Early-twentieth-century American films like *Gone with the Wind* (1939), starring Vivien Leigh and Clark Gable, and *The Little Colonel* (1935), starring Shirley Temple and Black actor and

Bill "Bojangles" Robinson and Shirley Temple in The Little Colonel, *1935.*

dancer Bill "Bojangles" Robinson, depict Black people as entertaining caretakers for white children and young adults. These images of happy-go-lucky Black servants were rooted in the false narrative that Blacks had been happy to be enslaved to white people in the years preceding the end of slavery in the United States. Some stereotypical Black characters still remain in American movies and television shows even today.

Millions of People Are Alive Today Thanks to an Eighteenth-Century Enslaved Man Whose Name Meant "Useful"

Most children in the United States today get a series of shots filled with powerful vaccines to protect them from dangerous diseases like polio, measles, mumps, and rubella. Vaccination is a type of *inoculation,* which means introducing a substance into a person's body in order to build up that person's immunity to a disease.

What you probably don't know is that it was a Black man named Onesimus who introduced the idea of inoculation to the British colonies three centuries ago!

It was a scary time. Smallpox was ravaging much of the world and had finally made its way to Boston. The colonists were terrified of the highly contagious virus, which caused fever, fatigue, and an itchy and unsightly rash that oozed pus from the skin. People often died from the disease, and those who survived were left with ugly permanent scars.

But in 1716, Onesimus (whose name comes from an ancient Greek word meaning "useful") told his owner, Cotton Mather, that back in his homeland in Africa, he had undergone a treatment that prevented him from catching the deadly disease.

The procedure Onesimus underwent was unconventional, to say the least. Pus from an active sore of a person infected with smallpox was rubbed into an open wound on Onesimus's body so that a tiny amount of the virus could seep into his system. Onesimus claimed that the procedure protected him from full infection with the virus. He believed it could save the lives of many other people as well.

What Onesimus was suggesting was not only unheard of among the colonists, it was scary! Mather, a vocal Puritan pastor who believed Africans were backward and inferior to white people, had only the word of his slave that the procedure worked. But, desperate to find a weapon against the dangerous virus that threatened the lives of so many people, he considered the unconventional preventive measure.

In 1721, Mather enlisted the help of a local doctor named Zabdiel Boylston to put Onesimus's claims to the test. When word got out, Mather faced public outrage over his willingness to try advice given to him by a slave.

When the next smallpox outbreak threatened the lives of Boston residents, Boylston began inoculating members of his family, his slaves, and other willing local residents. Working quickly, Boylston inoculated 242 people with the virus. Of those he treated, only 6 died. The survival rate of those who had been inoculated was far higher than that of those who hadn't been.

Onesimus's treatment was a success! In the end, smallpox claimed the lives of 844 Bostonians that year, but the number could've been far higher had Mather and Boylston refused the advice of a Black man.

In the decades that followed, inoculation became more widespread. Eventually, in 1796, the English doctor Edward Jenner developed the smallpox vaccine, advancing the innovative technique Onesimus shared with Mather. The vaccine eventually wiped out smallpox altogether, and the world was declared free of the disease in 1980. Onesimus played a role in saving millions of lives.

• • •

WHAT WAS LIFE LIKE FOR ENSLAVED CHILDREN?

As noted earlier in this chapter, many enslaved people raised white children from birth through adolescence. This was especially true for Black women, who were forced to forsake their own children to care for white children.

Some enslaved children experienced similar fates when they were bought as "gifts" for white children their age. They were expected to serve as both caretakers and playmates for their white counterparts. Often these arrangements produced deep bonds between white and Black children, although plantation culture reinforced white supremacist behavior so that Black children always knew their place as enslaved people to their white "friends."

From the start, Black children were taught that they were inferior to white children. Even at birth, the needs of white babies outweighed theirs. While their mothers nursed the white babies in the Big House, Black babies were forced to drink cow's milk from "suck-bottles."

This practice had negative health implications for Black babies, who couldn't benefit from the fortifying nutrients found in their mothers' breast milk. Most babies born to enslaved mothers had low birth weights to begin with, so being denied the chance to nurse from their mothers only increased their susceptibility to diseases and other ailments. During slavery, Black babies had a mortality rate as high as 50 percent—meaning half of all newborns born to enslaved mothers died.

If that wasn't devastating enough, those babies who did survive rarely had the opportunity to bond with their mothers during those important developmental months. That's because lactating Black women had to divide their time between nursing white babies and carrying out their labor-intense duties in the field or inside the Big House as cooks or maids.

Growing up as an enslaved child bore little resemblance to having a healthy childhood. In many ways, enslaved children were regarded as mini versions of adult slaves. While most children didn't have the labor responsibilities of enslaved adults, slave owners nevertheless regarded them as property. The owners wanted to invest only enough money in a child to guarantee the child would return a profit to them once he or she matured to adolescence. In other words, slave owners valued enslaved children only in terms of their future contributions to the plantation force.

Children were left to their own devices when their parents and other family members were in the fields or working in the Big House. Sometimes an elder enslaved person who was no longer able to carry out his or her grueling tasks would watch the enslaved children while the enslaved parents worked from sunup to sundown. In other instances, older children tended to the younger children until their parents returned at the end of the workday.

Like other boys and girls, enslaved children used their imaginations to pass the time. But unlike their white counterparts, they didn't have store-bought dolls or toys to stave off boredom. They had to make up their own games for entertainment.

You may have played tag with your friends. Enslaved children made up similar games of chase, but those unlucky players who got tagged would be "whipped" by the other players. Enslaved children learned and imitated the slave culture they were born into, and they realized early on the penalties of bad behavior, with running away being the worst offense. Just as small children are taught not to touch hot stoves or to go near fire, enslaved children were indoctrinated into slave customs not only by their parents and other adults but also by observing the oppressive system they had the misfortune to be born into.

We do not have accurate information regarding the regularity with which enslaved children were beaten, and that's probably because they didn't have as much interaction with white overseers and plantation hands as adults did, since they were not part of the plantation workforce. However, from slave narratives and twentieth-century interviews with formerly enslaved people, we know that enslaved children were beaten by white people for even the slightest infractions—even the playful antics children are known to enjoy.

Although whipping children was not a practice Africans brought with them to North America, some enslaved parents also severely punished their own children. They developed the practice because they knew firsthand the terror and pain of the slave master's lash, and they did all they could to teach their children to be good and respectful to avoid the white man's wrath, sometimes including physical punishment. But enslaved children were like other children and were bound to get into mischief at some point! When this happened, they might be beaten by their parents, relatives, or other older, watchful enslaved people to teach them valuable lessons about discipline and to prevent even worse punishment if they acted out under the ever-observant eyes of white people.

Some concerned Black parents today continue to use physical discipline in hopes of preventing altercations between their children and white people, or between their children and police. The fear is that, in the event of any kind of fight, Black children will be seen as second-class citizens or even criminals.

NAMING AND SELF-DETERMINATION

Remember the seafaring Black Jacks we learned about in Chapter 1? Paul Cuffe, a Black man from Massachusetts, is another example of a successful and courageous mariner.

Given the name Paul Slocum at birth, Cuffe was born in 1759 in southern Massachusetts. His father, Kofi Slocum, was a farmer who had once been enslaved. His mother, Ruth Moses, was a member of the Indigenous Wampanoag tribe.

The name Kofi is an Ashanti boys' name meaning

"born on Friday." The Ashanti tribe hails from Ghana, West Africa, so we have some evidence of Cuffe's African roots. After his father died, Cuffe changed his surname from Slocum to Cuffe, a close English spelling of his father's name, Kofi.

Cuffe became a sea captain and an entrepreneur who built and owned a fleet of his own ships and traveled with a crew consisting of other free Black men. But he was also an outspoken advocate for Black people, believing that they were entitled to the same rights as white people. He felt his rights were violated when his ship and its cargo of imported goods were detained by U.S. customs, so Cuffe took up the matter with the top man in charge: President James Madison! While it wasn't customary for everyday citizens to meet with the president of the United States in person, on May 2, 1812, this determined sea captain had an audience with him. At the end of their meeting, having heard Cuffe's petition, President Madison ordered that his ship and cargo be released.

During their time together, Madison questioned Cuffe about a growing interest in Black emigration to the Sierra Leone colony established for newly freed slaves. Cuffe, like many future Black activists and advocates, felt a strong kinship with Africa and dreamed of establishing settlements and trade opportunities between African Americans and their African kinsmen across the Atlantic Ocean.

Paul Cuffe's decision to take on his father's African name also reflects prevailing resistance to slavery and subjugation by white people. Slave traders and owners wanted to strip enslaved people of their former identities. One of the first steps of breaking enslaved people was to assign them new Anglo, French, Portuguese, Dutch, or Spanish names, depending on which slave-trading empire they fell victim to.

For enslaved Africans who had been taken from their homelands, their families, and everything they knew, being forced to take on a new name they perhaps couldn't even pronounce was disorienting and devastating. But many Africans refused to take on the new names assigned to them. They refused to answer when called by their European names, or they secretly held on to their given names among other slaves. Even many who did eventually accept their new names held on to their African names as well, and passed memories of them down throughout their family lines by oral tradition.

Firsthand oral histories of the last living enslaved people, as well as some slave narratives, document their African names, and in some cases the given names of their African ancestors, if they remembered them.

White people and their African captives recognized the importance of naming. To name a thing is to give it meaning. The ability to name a person, such as a child, endows the namer with authority and influence over the person being named. Even today, many African cultures take naming of children very seriously. For them, naming endows children with the necessary spiritual essence to guide them successfully through life. For those stolen Africans trafficked through the transatlantic slave trade, their names tied them to their people, their culture, and their destinies.

But white people not only replaced slaves' tribal names with new names; they also took the right to name their children away from them. A mother and father might look at their newborn child and decide to call her Ayodele (which means "joy enters the house"), while the slave master would name the baby girl Emma or Roberta depending upon his own ethnic heritage. In doing so, the slave owner reinforced all power over the couple and their helpless baby. In many cases, slave owners gave only a first name.

Still, Black people resisted the all-consuming nature of slave culture and found a way to take back some of their power through the use of nicknames, which were endowed with meaning and ancestral connections. In some instances the nicknames were African words and terms enslaved people recalled from their former lives. Other people gave their children the names of their African forebears as nicknames as a way to maintain connections to their ancestors. Once freed, the formerly enslaved would add a surname as an act of self-determination and, in some instances, by taking the name of the plantation where they had once been enslaved to show where they were from.

LET'S THINK ABOUT THIS:

1. How did enslaved people create a new culture in America?

2. How did plantation life contribute to the poor health of enslaved people?

3. Why did enslaved parents see punishing their children as a way to protect them from the violent punishment by slave owners and plantation overseers?

CHAPTER 5

THE AMERICAN REVOLUTION AND SLAVE-OWNING FOUNDING FATHERS

S o far, we have covered just how enslaved Black Africans and their American-born enslaved descendants were the labor force that built the Northern and Southern colonies of North America. Some of these very same Black people took up arms alongside white people who subjugated them in the fight for independence from England. Still others fought for England, hoping their allegiance might win their liberation if the British Crown was victorious.

There were thousands on both sides! By some estimates, upward of eight thousand free and enslaved Black men served on the battlegrounds for American independence. Another twenty thousand fought for England. No matter which side they chose to fight for, enslaved people and free Black people who fought in the war between the colonists and the British Crown were betting that the victors would set them free.

Some of the brave enslaved people who became soldiers for the redcoats gambled on allegiance to the British Crown and won their freedom. Well, sort of. After their defeat, the British Loyalists recorded the names, birthdates, and dates of escape of some three thousand enslaved people who ran away and joined their cause in the Inspection Roll of Negroes, more commonly called the Book of Negroes. In 1783, they granted those listed in the book freedom and safe passage to Nova Scotia in Canada.

That would've been a happy ending for the runaways who had joined the Loyalists, except that once they arrived in Nova Scotia, they had very little else but freedom with which to make a life in a new place.

Many others—namely those who joined the Patriots, as the revolutionaries called themselves—gambled and lost. Though the Black soldiers were on the winning side of the war, the white people who had just thrown off British rule doubled down on their tyranny over the very enslaved people who had helped them to victory.

It didn't matter to them that so many Black men

had risked their lives to support their cause for independence. They still believed Black people were inferior and not entitled to the same liberty and rights they had just established for themselves.

The Black men who served in the American Revolution didn't just fight. They contributed in many capacities on both sides, serving valiantly from the very beginning.

Of those who did fight, a Black man named Crispus Attucks was one of the most important. Both of Attucks's parents were enslaved. His father was African and his mother was an Indigenous Nantick of the Wampanoag tribal territories. Like his parents, Attucks spent his youth in bondage, but in 1750, at the age of twenty-seven, Attucks escaped the custody of his owner, William Brown, and was never recaptured.

As an adult, Attucks was a towering man who stood over six feet tall. His physical stature would come in handy when he struck the first blow in defense of the American Revolution.

Crispus Attucks, the first person killed in the American Revolution.

By 1770, Attucks was working as a sailor on whaling ships and as a rope maker, which came in handy in the port of Boston, where many ships were docked. These were some of the few jobs available to free Black men like Attucks, and they suddenly found themselves competing with British soldiers, who were paid meager wages for their service to the British Crown. Needing additional income to survive, British soldiers went after the part-time jobs that Black men depended on. Political tensions weren't just rising between the colonists and Great Britain; they were also mounting in the streets of Boston over competition for these jobs.

As tensions rose to a fever pitch, Attucks struck out against British soldiers. He threw the first punch in what would become a violent melee between colonial seamen and British soldiers known as the Boston Massacre. By the time the skirmish ended, five of the men fighting the British soldiers had been killed. Attucks was the first one to die and is thought to be the first person to die in the American Revolution.

Days after the Boston Massacre, Attucks and the other four men who died were given a hero's send-off. Their bodies lay in state for three days in Boston's Faneuil Hall, a meeting hall and marketplace where thousands of viewers stopped and paid their respects.

By some estimates, half the city's population came out to pay tribute to Attucks and his fellow fallen. Only in his death did white people respect and recognize Crispus Attucks's humanity.

As the American Revolution continued, formerly enslaved people played critical strategic roles as *minutemen*—trained militia ready to fight at a moment's notice—and even spies! In many of the war's crucial battles, Black soldiers helped turn the tide in favor of the American Patriots. Take, for instance, Peter Salem, a formerly enslaved man who emerged as a valiant asset during one of the earliest and most important skirmishes between the Patriots and British soldiers, known as the Battle of Bunker Hill, in 1775.

While they were eventually defeated at Bunker Hill, the Patriots killed many more enemy soldiers than they lost, demonstrating that they were a formidable force to be reckoned with, and not simply an unskilled militia. And it was Peter Salem, a Black man, who struck down the Crown's Major John Pitcairn as he scaled the Patriots' makeshift fort in a show of victory. Despite their loss, the Patriots were proud of the strength they had exhibited, and Salem was immortalized in 1786 when his image was included in a famous painting of the battle.

Black Patriots were also instrumental in carrying

out covert operations during the war as spies and even double agents. They played important strategic roles that white men couldn't.

One good example is an enslaved man who served as a valuable spy for the Patriots: James Armistead Lafayette (who took on his second surname after the war, in honor of the famous general under whom he served). With permission from his owner, James Armistead pretended that he was a runaway enslaved man seeking refuge and wanting to serve the British Crown in order to gain his freedom. Believing his story, British soldiers took him in and put him to work doing low-level jobs. Eventually they began tapping into his knowledge of the geographic area, hoping to gain a strategic advantage over the Patriots.

Armistead gave them bits of information to convince them of his loyalty, and eventually they asked him to spy on the Patriots! He was getting

James Armistead Lafayette, right, served as a spy for the Patriots in the American Revolution.

good at being a spy, so he accepted the task of being a double agent. But he stayed loyal to the Patriots the whole time. When he brought back information to the British, he earned more of their trust, and he fed everything he learned about them to the Patriots while giving the British bogus information about the Patriots' next moves.

Armistead's actions gave the Patriots key information, such as details about the British war headquarters and specifics about imminent British reinforcements, which helped General George Washington and his troops defeat the British in the Siege of Yorktown.

In addition to Black men serving as soldiers and spies, there were whole infantries almost entirely made up of Black men who fought in the American Revolution. In 1778, Rhode Island made it legal for both free and enslaved Black people to serve in combat.

Of the many Black men who stood up to serve, some were assigned to the First Rhode Island Regiment, a small but mighty fighting unit. The regiment consisted of roughly 130 men, most of them Black, who were lauded for their fighting spirit and success on the battlefield. In May 1781, they fought to the death protecting their commander, Colonel Christopher Greene. By some accounts, members of the regiment shielded Greene with their bodies to protect him. In the end their valor couldn't save him, but they died fighting nevertheless.

Countless men like Crispus Attucks, Peter Salem, James Armistead Lafayette, and the members of the First Rhode Island Regiment helped defeat the British. Without their help, it is quite possible that the Patriots wouldn't have won the war, and their independence as a nation.

THE FOUNDING FATHERS WANTED FREEDOM, BUT ONLY FOR THEMSELVES

As the Founding Fathers celebrated their independence from Britain and developed the framework for the new nation, they were also grappling with the issue of slavery. Although they wanted freedom from British rule, they only wanted it for themselves. The sad irony is that these freedom seekers were guilty of an even more dastardly form of tyranny than their British rulers in the enslavement and inhumane treatment of human beings.

Their newfound freedom, they decided, would not be extended to slaves. Instead, when the U.S. Constitution was finally ratified in 1788, it included language that would affect Black life for close to

WHICH
U.S. PRESIDENTS
OWNED SLAVES
& HOW MANY DID THEY OWN?

George
WASHINGTON
577

Thomas
JEFFERSON
600+

James
MADISON
100+

James
MONROE
178

Andrew
JACKSON
150+

Martin
VAN BUREN
1

William Henry
HARRISON
11

John
TYLER
70

James K.
POLK
59

Zachary
TAYLOR
131+

Andrew
JOHNSON
8

Ulysses S.
GRANT
1

two and a half centuries: "three fifths of all other Persons."

Known as the Three-Fifths Compromise, the clause was meant to ensure fair congressional representation based upon population size. On the one hand, if the entire enslaved population in the South were counted as part of the population, Southern states would have a huge representative advantage over Northern states. Northern delegates would not agree to that. However, they couldn't ignore or discount enslaved people outright, so in the end, they compromised by counting only three of every five enslaved people in the census.

Even worse, after Black Patriots fought alongside them in the Revolutionary War, the Founding Fathers turned their backs on them and all Black people, free and enslaved alike, living in the colonies, by creating laws to prevent them from ever being truly free. In 1793, Congress passed the first Fugitive Slave Act, which meant that runaway enslaved people could be hunted down like animals, and if found in free states, they could be sent back to captivity.

You're probably wondering how some states came to be "free states" and others "slave states." Well, as the United States expanded and took on new territories, political leaders wanted to ensure that there was a balance of free and slave states to protect states' rights and the interests of American citizens. By 1820, there were eleven slave states: Maryland, Virginia, Kentucky, Tennessee, North Carolina, South Carolina, Georgia, Alabama, Mississippi, Louisiana, and Delaware. And there were eleven free states: Vermont, New Hampshire, New York, Massachusetts, Rhode

Island, Connecticut, New Jersey, Pennsylvania, Ohio, Indiana, and Illinois.

That year, under a law called the Missouri Compromise, Missouri was admitted as a slave state and Maine was added as a free state. In 1850, there was another compromise, which admitted California as a free state and left Utah and New Mexico free to decide on their own. But the Compromise of 1850 also included the second Fugitive Slave Act, which called for harsh punishment and penalties for runaways and allies who helped them escape. The new Fugitive Slave Act made it even more difficult for enslaved people to not only escape to freedom but stay free once they made it to free states; prior to 1850, free states welcomed runaways and granted them legal protections.

This may also be hard to believe, but of the ten American presidents who owned slaves, eight did so while serving in the highest office in the nation.

It's true. In fact, of the earliest American presidents, only John Adams, the second president, and his son, John Quincy Adams, the sixth president, opposed slavery and thus were not slaveholders. For the others, the precept from the Declaration of Independence that "all men are created equal" did not extend to Black people, on whose backs the country they led was built. Even the country's two highest seats of power—the White

House and the U.S. Capitol Building—were built using enslaved Black people's labor!

The Declaration of Independence was adopted by the Second Continental Congress meeting in Philadelphia, Pennsylvania, on July 4, 1776. It gave voice to the colonies' desire for independence from the kingdom of Great Britain, but the truth is that the majority of the signers of the Declaration were slave owners—forty-one out of the fifty-six, to be exact. At the time of the Second Continental Congress in 1776, seventeen of the fifty-six delegates owned over a thousand enslaved people collectively.

These political leaders didn't see the contradiction between the guiding principles of the Declaration and their involvement with slavery. Their blindness set the tone for generations of American political leaders and everyday citizens to extol the virtues of "life, liberty, and the pursuit of happiness" while oppressing Black people at the same time.

GEORGE WASHINGTON AND THE GREAT ESCAPE OF ONA "ONEY" JUDGE

George Washington and his wife, Martha, owned three hundred enslaved people at their home, Mount

Vernon, Virginia, across the Potomac River from what became the nation's capital, Washington, D.C. Many of these were "dower slaves" (that is, inherited slaves) whom Martha received from the estate of her first husband, Daniel Parke Custis, when he died.

Washington himself became a slave owner at the tender age of eleven years old when his father, Augustine, passed away. Upon his father's death, young George was bequeathed 280 acres of land and ten slaves.

Although George Washington expressed conflicting feelings about slavery throughout his life, he ended up owning 123 men, women, and children. And at the time of his death, he and Martha together owned a total of 317 enslaved people who were living and working at Mount Vernon.

While serving as the sitting president, he had at least ten enslaved people laboring in the presidential residences, first in New York and then in Philadelphia: Ona, Hercules, Moll, Giles, Austin, Paris, Richmond, Joe, Christopher Sheels, and Richard Lee. These enslaved people faced separation from their loved ones back at Mount Vernon when the Washingtons occupied the presidential residences.

While George Washington believed there were gentler ways to maintain order among enslaved people, he ultimately authorized the violent disciplinary tactics enforced by his overseers. His moral compromise was to declare in his will that his enslaved people should be freed upon his death. This meant that Martha had the responsibility of carrying out her husband's wishes, since he passed away before she did. Fearing that the enslaved workers might cause her physical harm, she respected her late husband's wishes and set them free. In December 1800, Martha Washington signed a deed of manumission—release from slavery—for the late president's slaves, a transaction that is recorded in the Fairfax County, Virginia, court records. They would finally be emancipated on January 1, 1801. Unfortunately, this act of manumission did not extend to all the enslaved people the Washingtons owned. Under the terms of Daniel Custis's will, Martha did not own outright the people she inherited; upon her death, they were passed down to her children and grandchildren. Those dower slaves were the vast majority of the Black population at Mount Vernon.

Although his writings convey that he had mixed feelings about slavery and the violent treatment of his and Martha's human property, George Washington was resolute in his pursuit of one enslaved person in particular: Ona "Oney" Judge, a runaway dower slave, who escaped and evaded capture and return.

Oney was the daughter of an enslaved woman named Betty, a seamstress living at Mount Vernon. Oney's father was a white man named Andrew Judge. A tailor by trade, Judge himself was an indentured servant also living at Mount Vernon. Although his life and living conditions may have been harsher than those of nonservants, he was not the property of the Washingtons.

As a little girl, Oney was brought into the family domicile, possibly to become the playmate of Martha Washington's granddaughter Nelly Custis, who was similar in age and staying at Mount Vernon. Oney would go on to become Martha's body servant, or personal maid. In this capacity, Oney accompanied her mistress on shopping excursions and visits to some of the other colonies.

In 1789, the U.S. capital city was New York, and the Washingtons brought Oney with them to serve in the presidential residence there. The following year, the capital location was changed to Philadelphia, and when the Washingtons moved to their new home, Oney, along with seven other enslaved people, once again accompanied them.

But Pennsylvania had abolished slavery in 1780, which meant that by keeping enslaved people on the presidential property, the Washingtons were breaking the law! "An Act for the Gradual Abolition of Slavery" decreed that any enslaved person living in the state for six consecutive months must be freed.

In order to appear compliant with the state law, the Washingtons regularly rotated out the enslaved people who lived with them: they would send some of their servants back to Mount Vernon after they'd been in Philadelphia just short of six months, bring different enslaved people to replace them, and then repeat the process after another just-under-six-months stint. This allowed them to skirt the law until a 1788 amendment to the Pennsylvania law prohibited such behavior.

For Oney, life was very different in Philadelphia than it had been at Mount Vernon, because slavery was generally frowned upon there. Abolitionists actively and openly worked in opposition to slavery by holding public meetings and printing pamphlets that exposed its horrors. Free African Americans in the city outnumbered enslaved people by six to one!

Upon arrival, Oney was given money to attend

plays, shows, and circus performances. She also accompanied Martha to social events and got to dress in fine clothing, such as high-quality stockings, bonnets, and dresses. These indulgences gave the appearance of freedom, but in reality she still wasn't free at all.

Seeing people who looked like her living freely ignited something in Oney. With the help of newfound friends and the abolitionist community, Oney Judge made up her mind to break out of captivity. The perfect opportunity presented itself on May 20, 1796. While the Washingtons made preparations to return to Mount Vernon, she seized her chance to make a daring escape.

Later in her life, Oney described for a writer how she devised her plan: "Whilst they were packing up to go to Virginia, I was packing to go, I didn't know where; for I knew that if I went back to Virginia, I should never get my liberty. I had friends among the colored people of Philadelphia, had my things carried there beforehand, and left Washington's house while they were eating dinner."

Oney seized her opportunity to flee farther north to Portsmouth, New Hampshire, and boarded a one-masted sailboat, or sloop, named the *Nancy*. With the aid of the captain, John Bowles, who had the reputation of being sympathetic to runaway slaves, she was bound for freedom.

The Washingtons were furious about Oney's escape. They didn't outright own her since she was a part of the Custis dower, so her escape meant that they would in fact owe the remaining Custis heirs for her loss. And Martha believed Oney "was brought up more like a child than treated like a Servant" by the Washingtons. It never occurred to Martha that Oney longed to have what every free citizen experienced—life, liberty, and the pursuit of happiness.

The ad placed by George Washington in the Philadelphia Gazette *and* Daily Advertiser *offering ten dollars for the capture of Oney Judge.*

Several days later, advertisements offering a ten-dollar reward for the capture and return of the young woman ran in the *Philadelphia Gazette and Daily Advertiser* and *Claypoole's American Daily Advertiser.* The Washingtons used their power and influence to try to secure Oney's return to their custody.

Persistent in their pursuit of the runaway, they enlisted the help of Oliver Wolcott Jr., secretary of the treasury. Wolcott, in turn, entrusted Joseph Whipple, the collector of customs in Portsmouth, to find and recapture Oney.

Whipple was only partially successful in his endeavor. To entrap Oney, Whipple ran a fake ad for a domestic servant. That part of his scheme worked; Oney showed up in search of money to support herself. During their meeting, Whipple revealed his true motive and interrogated the frightened but savvy girl, who tried to negotiate the best circumstances for her impending return to slavery. Through Whipple, she agreed to return to captivity if the Washingtons agreed to her freedom upon both of their deaths.

George Washington was livid. He responded to Whipple in a letter stating the following:

> *To enter into such a compromise, as* she *suggested to* you, *is totally inadmissible. . . . [I]t would neither be politic or just, to reward unfaithfulness with a premature preference [of freedom]; and thereby discontent, beforehand, the minds of all her fellow Servants; who by their steady adherence, are far more deserving than herself, of favor.*

With the help of her friends in Portsmouth, Oney was able to evade recapture on a number of occasions. Once, she was spotted by one of Nelly Custis's childhood friends, Elizabeth Langdon, who was the daughter of New Hampshire senator John Langdon. And two years after she was detained and interrogated by Joseph Whipple, Oney was to avoid recapture once again. This time, Burwell Bassett Jr., Washington's nephew, traveled to New Hampshire in hopes of securing Oney's return to the Washingtons. Oney was alerted to Bassett's plans by the Langdons. Armed with the news of Bassett's intentions, she was hidden by her friends.

Eventually the Washingtons stopped searching and Oney was able to settle down and make a life for herself in Portsmouth. She married a sailor named Jack Staines, and they had three children together. Sadly, Staines died seven years into their marriage. Oney and her children lived in poverty and eventually moved in with the Jacks, a free Black family living in Greenland, New Hampshire. Oney Judge Staines outlived her children (her daughters both dying in their thirties, her son at an unknown time), and died in 1848 at the age of seventy-three.

You might think that Oney's life as a free woman was harder than the life she lived with the

Washingtons, or that hers isn't a story with a happy ending. However, near the end of her life, when asked if she had any regrets escaping captivity by the Washingtons, she replied: "No, I am free, and have, I trust been made a child of God by the means."

THOMAS JEFFERSON

Thomas Jefferson left an indelible mark on American history—one that demonstrates the complexity of the problem of race in American society. Even today, Jefferson is regarded as one of the nation's greatest statesmen, political minds, and visionaries for democracy and freedom. Through his prolific writing and astute political leadership, he left a monumental legacy that helped shape the moral consciousness of the country.

One of Jefferson's

THOMAS JEFFERSON,
Vice President of the U.S.

A portrait of Thomas Jefferson painted between 1797 and 1800.

talents was his gift for writing, which is most evident in the Declaration of Independence and in the vast collection of books and papers that documents his experiences and sentiments on many topics, including the right of men to be free. In a letter to the English statesman David Hartley, he wrote the following about the importance of self-determination: "I have no fear that the result of our experiment will be that men may be trusted to govern themselves without a master."

While Jefferson believed that white men should be able to govern themselves, he also believed in their right to seize the freedom of Black and Indigenous men, women, and children. In fact, he was the mastermind behind some of the bloodiest sieges that left many Indigenous people dead and their native lands stolen.

Jefferson was born into a family and society that thrived upon the labor of enslaved people. Although he himself bought fewer than twenty enslaved people during his life, he inherited around two hundred. As those enslaved people bore children, the total number of people he owned over the years grew to around six hundred. They were responsible for farming, building his beloved Monticello estate, and running household affairs. Many of them were your age, or even younger.

In "Notes on the State of Virginia," Jefferson described slavery as forcing "tyranny and depravity" upon master and slave alike, meaning that slavery negatively affected both enslaved people and the white people who held them captive. But recognizing the injustice of forcing other humans into bondage for free labor was not enough to stop him from participating in the inhumane practice. It remains a paradox that Jefferson created one of the most masterful declarations for freedom ever written and simultaneously deprived Black people of that very same freedom.

Jefferson's behavior was particularly abhorrent in his treatment of one of his enslaved women, Sally Hemings, on whom he forced a sexual relationship. Sadly, this was a grotesque reality Sally was already accustomed to: Her mother, Elizabeth, was an enslaved woman, and her father, John Wayles, was Elizabeth's owner. Both Elizabeth and Sally endured unwanted advances from their masters, and each of the women bore their masters' children. John Wayles also had four daughters by his first two wives; the oldest, Martha, married Thomas Jefferson.

Sally was born in 1773. A year later, she and the rest of her enslaved family moved to Monticello as part of Martha Wayles Jefferson's inheritance when her father died. There, Sally would eventually become nursemaid, or personal servant, to Jefferson's young daughter, Maria, who in fact was her niece, since Sally and Martha were half sisters.

While Sally shared the same ancestry as Martha and Maria, the similarities between them stopped there. Sally's life as an enslaved girl and then woman wasn't anything like the charmed lives the Jefferson women experienced.

At age fourteen, Sally accompanied Maria to Paris. There she learned French and received training in needlework and dressmaking so that she could fulfill her duties as Maria's lady's maid.

Living in Paris had its benefits for Sally. First, she was reunited with one of her older brothers—James— whom Thomas Jefferson had brought over earlier to learn the culinary skills associated with French cuisine to impress dignitaries and other guests in America upon their return home. Second, Sally was able to move about freely in France, and Jefferson actually paid her wages for her work.

However, Paris also had its drawbacks for Sally. Sometime during the twenty-six months she was there, Thomas Jefferson, who was thirty years her senior, forced the young girl into a sexual relationship, and by the time she was sixteen years old, she was pregnant.

Although she was just a child herself, Sally knew all too well the horrors of slavery and what lay ahead for her unborn child. She was also very intelligent. So when Jefferson demanded that the teenage girl return to Monticello with him at the end of his stay, she brokered a deal.

Sally agreed to return with Jefferson only after he guaranteed that she and her unborn child would be granted special privileges, including freedom from hard labor and a promise that none of her relatives, including any future children, would be sold off, so that her family could remain intact. This was truly an extraordinary agreement between an enslaved person and a slave owner.

In total, Sally gave birth to six of Thomas Jefferson's children. She would see two of them die before they reached the age of three. However, because of her arrangement with Jefferson, she had the freedom to raise her own children, which in late-eighteenth-century Virginia was a privilege enjoyed almost exclusively by white people.

Jefferson freed Sally's surviving children, Harriet, Beverly, Madison, and Eston, in adulthood. Harriet and Beverly were allowed to leave Monticello first, in 1822, followed by Madison and Eston, who were granted freedom in Jefferson's will four years later.

Thomas Jefferson died in 1826 without ever granting Sally her freedom. Maria allowed Sally Hemings to leave Monticello to live with her children, but she never saw the legal light of freedom for herself. The facts surrounding Sally Hemings's life are recounted in the writing of her son Madison, who documented his mother's story as a testament to all that she endured.

SLAVERY WAS A COMPLICATED TOPIC AMONG EARLY AMERICAN LEADERS

Like Thomas Jefferson, Congress as a whole wrestled with varying issues surrounding slavery. But don't go thinking that members of Congress suffered from a crisis of conscience around the buying, selling, and enslavement of humans. That would be wrong.

In reality, in the late 1700s there was growing sentiment among Americans and in Britain that the slave trade was a human rights violation—after Britain spent decades transporting upward of 3 million enslaved Africans to the Caribbean, the United States, and other countries for profit. During the 1787 Constitutional Convention, congressional leaders agreed to restrict the slave trade, but the Act Prohibiting the

Importation of Slaves wasn't passed until 1807 and didn't go into effect until 1808.

Nevertheless, Britain's change of heart on the issue of slavery and the mounting anti-slavery movement from within were enough to pressure American political leaders to pass the Slave Trade Act of 1800, which made it illegal for Americans to participate in the sale and importation of enslaved people between nations. This same law gave the United States the right to detain any ships found to be carrying enslaved people for sale and to retain ownership of the vessel's cargo.

While it's true that the United States ended its involvement in the transatlantic slave trade in 1808, that did not mean that slavery and the bustling slave market ended here. In fact, the 1807 act made it easier for American slave traders in places like Virginia to make more money by selling their enslaved people to Southern plantation owners. Without competition from foreign slave traders, American slave traders grew richer. The United States didn't really need enslaved people from Africa anymore, because the people they'd already enslaved continued to reproduce, giving them a steady stream of humans for sale. Ultimately, the 1807 act didn't change anything for enslaved people.

SLAVERY IN THE WAKE OF AMERICAN EXPANSIONISM

Have you ever heard of Lewis and Clark? They were two young, scrappy guys Thomas Jefferson commissioned as part of the Corps of Discovery—a special unit of the U.S. Army established by Thomas Jefferson to explore the vast terrain acquired through the Louisiana Purchase in 1803. William Clark and Merriweather Lewis met in the army, and when Lewis enlisted Clark's help in the expedition, Clark brought along York, a slave.

The motley expedition crew included skilled soldiers, interpreters, and rowers who knew how to navigate the dangerous waters ahead. York was the only enslaved person on the journey. The Indigenous Nez Perce people and the Russian trappers and seamen they encountered were intrigued by his six-foot stature and dark skin. In these instances, Lewis and Clark encouraged their curiosity and allowed them to poke and prod poor York, at times to the point of bleeding. In one incident, a white crew member threw sand at him, supposedly in jest, and York almost lost his eye as a result. But over the course of the twenty-eight-month expedition, York proved to

A statue of York, left, with Lewis and Clark and Lewis's dog Seaman, in Great Falls, Montana.

be valiant, resourceful, and loyal. When food was low, he scouted for game using guns the crew brought along.

When Lewis and Clark returned from their harrowing journey, all the white men were rewarded for their valor. They were given money and land, among other recognitions.

York received none of these. He wasn't manumitted upon return from the expedition he never signed up for in the first place. Out on the trail, York had been given responsibilities and some sense of freedom most enslaved people never dreamed of. He even carried a firearm like the white men on the journey. Despite York's commitment and courage, and despite having freed other enslaved people in the past, Clark refused to grant York his freedom.

In the face of such injustice, York spoke up for himself and asked for his freedom based on his life-long servitude to Clark and meritorious contributions to the expedition. Still, Clark refused.

Undeterred, York made another petition: this time to be hired out to a Kentucky planter so that he could be near his wife. Hiring out enslaved people to work on other plantations was not uncommon, but Clark was becoming angry and growing tired of his slave's requests. He eventually agreed—but he sent York to work for a Kentucky plantation owner who was notorious for his violent treatment of slaves.

It's unlikely that the arrangement was like anything York had hoped for. At the end of his one-year stint in Kentucky, he returned to Clark's service in Missouri, undoubtedly missing his wife. In letters to his brother, Clark described severe beatings he had given the dutiful York, as well as his orders that York be sent farther south if he ever tried to escape during his time in Kentucky. Although York had faithfully served Clark for the better part of his entire life, Clark never truly recognized his humanity. Some twenty years later, he finally granted York his freedom. It isn't clear if York ever saw his wife again.

LET'S THINK ABOUT THIS:

1. Can people be great leaders but do bad things at the same time?

2. How do you think Oney Judge felt living among free Black people in New Hampshire?

3. Why do you think Thomas Jefferson never granted Sally Hemings her freedom?

4. In what ways did slavery force depravity on both slave owners and enslaved people?

CHAPTER 6

SLAVE RESISTANCE

S lave resistance took many forms.

From the beginning, some enslaved people flat-out refused to be subjugated. Some of the captive Africans, in defiance and desperation, jumped into the Atlantic Ocean during the Middle Passage rather than face their fate as enslaved people in an unknown land.

Other enslaved people recognized their own agency and used whatever means they had to protect themselves and their loved ones from the brutality and inhumane treatment that was commonplace during the arduous journey to America. Some devised cunning plans for escape and thwarted vigilante slave catchers who were always on the lookout for runaways.

Those who mustered up the courage to run away knew what might lie ahead for them: bloodhounds, bounty hunters, and possibly even betrayal by other enslaved people who knew of their plans. But even the uncertainty of reaching freedom didn't stop them from trying.

An overworked enslaved person might pretend to be sick to avoid the strenuous work of picking cotton, tobacco, or sugar, or cultivating rice in the swampy marshes of South Carolina from sunup to sundown. Others might load their sacks with rocks to make the weight of their daily quota of two hundred pounds of cotton.

Some defiant enslaved Africans either refused to learn English or resisted physical punishment by fighting back. In some instances, they destroyed property in retaliation for inhumane treatment.

Many enslaved people were more subtle and creative in their resistance. For example, some pretended to be dim-witted or incapable of carrying out strenuous chores or humiliating tasks such as flogging a fellow slave. By acting this way, they played on racist beliefs—that Black people were inferior to white people and lacked intellect—to get out of back-breaking tasks, even if it was only for a short while.

A favored enslaved person might act devoted by day but help plot an insurrection by night. An enslaved person in charge of preparing the master's meals might slowly poison him over time.

Enslaved people were forced to smile and act happy when guests of the plantation master visited. Sometimes they were forced to smile after enduring violent beatings or witnessing the severe punishment of loved ones. They learned to survive by wearing different "masks" to hide their true feelings and take back some of their power from their oppressors. Slavery forced them to play many roles and wear many faces to protect the ones they loved and to stay alive.

Thirty years after the Thirteenth Amendment to the Constitution outlawed slavery throughout the United States, a Black poet named Paul Laurence Dunbar penned a poem that describes a behavior Black people employed during slavery, and still employ even today, to resist white supremacist violence in an attempt to stay alive:

WE WEAR THE MASK

We wear the mask that grins and lies,
It hides our cheeks and shades our eyes,—

This debt we pay to human guile;
With torn and bleeding hearts we smile,
And mouth with myriad subtleties.

Why should the world be over-wise,
In counting all our tears and sighs?
Nay, let them only see us, while
We wear the mask.

We smile, but, O great Christ, our cries
To thee from tortured souls arise.
We sing, but oh the clay is vile
Beneath our feet, and long the mile;
But let the world dream otherwise,
We wear the mask!

Desperate times sometimes led to desperate acts by long-suffering slaves. There are documented stories of enslaved people killing their owners or other white people in self-defense or revenge. Parents, siblings, husbands, and wives alike offered themselves up for beatings to shield the ones they loved from the sting of the whip. In one unfathomable situation, a desperate woman named Margaret Garner attempted to kill her children and then herself after suffering through years of enslavement, violence, and separation from friends and loved ones. Garner, her husband, and their small children escaped slavery in Kentucky, and when federal marshals tracked them down in Ohio, Garner did the unthinkable: she slit the throat of her two-year-old daughter, killing her, and wounded her remaining children. In her mind, death was her only recourse.

Alternatively, some enslaved people planned and participated in small- and large-scale insurrections, while others absconded in the dead of night, fleeing captivity. Still others attempted to make the law of the land work on their behalf.

Portrait of Mum Bett (also known as Elizabeth Freeman), the first enslaved person to file and win a freedom suit, painted by Susan Ridley Sedgwick, ca. 1812.

MUM BETT

The case of a plaintiff who, at the time, was known only as Bett is one early instance of enslaved people invoking the law to justify and secure their freedom. In 1773, Bett, an enslaved woman living in Sheffield, Massachusetts, overheard her master, John

Ashley, speaking with a group of colleagues about the Sheffield Declaration, which described "rights of man."

Bett, who had been enslaved since childhood, was so moved by the words she heard while serving the men and "keeping still and minding things," that nearly a decade later she enlisted the assistance of a lawyer to help her secure her freedom.

Bett decided to seek help from the lawyer after she experienced a violent assault at the hands of John Ashley's wife, Hannah. In a fit of anger, Hannah attempted to hit Bett's daughter, Lizzie, with a heated kitchen shovel. Bett tried to shield Lizzie and suffered a terrible wound.

For Bett, that was the last straw. After listening to Ashley and his friends talk so passionately about all men being born free, Bett felt that freedom extended to all people, including her.

Because of his anti-slavery leanings, the lawyer Theodore Sedgwick took on Bett's case, which also included a co-plaintiff, an enslaved man named Brom in the Ashley household; the 1781 case came to be known as *Brom & Bett v. J. Ashley.*

Sedgwick argued that Bett and Brom were being unlawfully enslaved by Ashley. That's because the 1780 Massachusetts Constitution decreed that all individuals were "born free and equal," which basically trumped Ashley's claim of ownership of Brom and Bett.

And guess what: The courts agreed! Bett and Brom were set free under the Massachusetts Constitution, *and* John Ashley had to pay them restitution—money for damages they'd sustained while enslaved—in the amount of "thirty shillings and costs." Bett, who chose the name Elizabeth Freeman for herself after she won her case, and who was also called Mum Bett (*Mum* being a title of respect), lived the rest of her days as a self-determined free woman and earned a living as a paid domestic servant, not as a slave. By 1807, she had purchased her own house and nearly eighteen acres of land, where she lived far into old age near her daughter, grandchildren, and great-grandchildren.

The success of this landmark court case established precedent—or guidance for future cases of the same nature—and eventually set the legal stage for the abolition of slavery in Massachusetts.

CHARLOTTE "LOTTIE" DUPUY

Charlotte "Lottie" Dupuy was another enslaved woman who tried to use the American legal system to turn the tables on her master and legally win her freedom. In

1829, Lottie was owned by the U.S. secretary of state, Henry Clay, who had purchased the young enslaved woman from James Condon, her former owner.

Prior to selling Lottie and her two children, Charles and Mary Ann, Condon promised to free the family in seventeen years. Lottie felt strongly that this agreement was legally binding and that it transferred to Clay when he purchased her from Condon. So she enlisted the help of local attorneys in Washington, D.C., to represent her when Clay's tenure as secretary of state ended and he was preparing to return to Kentucky. She sued Clay for her freedom and that of her children in the U.S. Circuit Court for the District of Columbia!

As the case proceeded, Lottie stayed in Washington, working for the next secretary of state, Martin Van Buren, who would later become vice president and then the eighth U.S. president. Unfortunately, the court ultimately denied Lottie's petition. Defiant to the very end, she refused to return to life as a slave. Lottie was imprisoned in a Virginia jail before being remanded to Clay's custody in Kentucky.

Henry Clay did eventually grant Lottie and her children their freedom—eleven years later. Lottie's husband, Aaron Dupuy, who was also owned by Clay, wouldn't get his manumission until another four years after that.

Interestingly enough, Clay was known as the "Great Pacificator" for his forward-thinking and creative approach to diplomacy and American economic advancements. He would go on to become one of the architects of the 1850 Compromise, which limited the expansion of slavery in the new territories the United States acquired through the Mexican-American War. Ironically, while Clay believed slavery was "this great evil . . . the darkest spot in the map of our country," he himself owned as many as sixty slaves.

Other enslaved people would go on to sue for their freedom, and like Lottie, most were unsuccessful. The most famous of these cases would be filed by an enslaved man named Dred Scott in 1846. The case would drag on for years, ending with the final 1857 Supreme Court verdict now known as the *Dred Scott* decision.

Scott sued on the grounds that his owner, John Emerson, had moved both him and his wife, Harriet, also enslaved by Emerson, from Missouri, which was a slave state, to the state of Illinois and then to Wisconsin Territory, both free, throughout his military commissions. At the time of Emerson's death, however, the members of his household, including Scott and his wife, were residing in Missouri once again.

Scott and his lawyers argued that Scott and Harriet had been freed once Emerson took them to free states. Ultimately, Chief Justice Roger Brooke Taney ruled that this didn't hold. The Scotts lost their fight in court. They wouldn't be freed until they were purchased and then freed by Taylor Blow, the son of the man who had sold Scott to John Emerson originally.

THE CASE OF THE *AMISTAD*

In August 1839, a ship called the *Amistad,* carrying captured Africans who had been sold into slavery in Cuba, was seized off the coast of Long Island, New York, by American authorities. Remember that in 1808, the United States officially banned the importation of enslaved people for sale in the country. But that didn't mean slavery ended or that it suddenly became illegal to buy and sell people. It just meant that Americans could no longer buy enslaved people from the European countries, which were making the most money in the slave trade. And this is why the case of the *Amistad* generated so much attention from people on both sides of the debate over slavery in the United States.

Aboard this particular ship were fifty-three Africans from Sierra Leone, along with Pedro Montes and José Ruiz, the two Spanish businessmen who had purchased the captives. The captives had heard stories about what happened to their kinsmen who were taken by white men and never returned home to their families. They were scared, desperate, and determined not to be slaves. So they fought back.

After they killed the ship's captain and cook, the rebels took over the ship and demanded that Montes and Ruiz take them back to Africa. But the slavers tricked them and steered the vessel northward instead, where they were spotted by the captain of a U.S. naval ship. The captain seized the ship and took everyone aboard, except Montes and Ruiz, to jail.

The African men were imprisoned and charged with the murders of the cook and the captain. But they were acquitted of the charges because they had been illegally transported across the Atlantic Ocean and into American waters. By transporting the Africans aboard the *Amistad* to the United States, Montes and Ruiz were actually breaking the law.

The court also ruled that the actions of the captive Africans were justified, since they were free people trying to defend themselves and escape captivity by Montes and Ruiz.

But that's not where the story ends. Even though the court ruled in favor of the African men, many white men still wanted to claim them. Montes and Ruiz argued that the men were their property; the naval captain claimed *he* had a "salvage" right to them along with the ship since he had discovered them in American waters; and even the country of Spain said it was entitled to the men, or at the very least payment for their value in the slave market!

No one cared about the African men who had been stolen from their homeland, whose families would never know what happened to them. That is, until white abolitionists heard about the case and believed it could be an effective tool to expose the depravity and evils of slavery and gain support for the anti-slavery cause.

The case went from the federal court to the district court, all the way to the Supreme Court, where the fifty-three African men were represented by none other than former U.S. president John Quincy Adams. Adams, who once said that the American Revolution would not be complete until all enslaved people were freed, evoked this sentiment and even that of the Declaration of Independence in his nine-hour defense of the men. Remember, he and his father, John Adams, were the lone outliers among the nation's first twelve presidents in that they did not own slaves.

After hearing Adams's argument, the Supreme Court ruled in favor of the Sierra Leonean men. In the end, Adams's passion and legal mind were the right combination to set the captives free!

By the time the case was closed, only thirty-five of

the courageous Amistad rebels were still alive. Some had lost their lives during the fated journey; others died in jail while awaiting and hoping for a favorable verdict in their case. The survivors who had once been kidnapped and shackled by their captors returned to their homeland as free men once again.

THE STONO REBELLION

Although white people managed to subjugate, brutalize, and otherwise violate the human rights of generations of enslaved people, the number of Black people in the United States, especially in the South, continued to grow. In places like the Carolina Low Country, Black people made up the majority of the population. Nevertheless, the physical, mental, and emotional shackles of slavery kept the masses of Black people—both enslaved and free—trapped in systemic oppression.

But even with the power and fear they wielded, white people were consumed with the thought that their enslaved people might rise up and strike back in retaliation for their lives in bondage.

This fear was fueled by stories of places like Fort Mosé. In 1804, when Haiti won its independence from France, in large part because of a rebellion by enslaved people, its status as the first free Black nation in the Americas became a beacon of hope and a rallying cry for enslaved people throughout the United States and South and Central America. In response, anxious slave owners and plantation overseers took great measures to control enslaved people through fear and intimidation. Overseers and other plantation officials policed enslaved people at gunpoint and used the constant threat of violence—flogging, branding, maiming, and other torture, including being torn limb from limb by dogs—to keep them in line.

The personal diaries, letters, and biographies of wealthy slave owners and other observers document this preoccupation with fear of slave insurrection. But large-scale slave rebellions were rare in the United States.

The largest slave rebellion in North American history took place on September 9, 1739 (more than half a century before the Haitian Revolution), when Jemmy, an enslaved man from Angola, orchestrated a slave insurrection along the Stono River, some twenty miles south of Charleston, South Carolina. Jemmy and his determined co-conspirators struck at the most opportune time: a Sunday morning when white people would be at church.

First they attacked a local store and seized firearms for the ensuing battle. Emboldened, the angry crew pillaged property, killing white people and forcing reluctant enslaved people to join their uprising along the way. Shouting "Liberty!" the band of freedom-seeking enslaved people marched toward Florida in hopes of finding refuge in Saint Augustine, the Spanish enclave of free Africans.

Soon the group of rebels had grown to include a hundred enslaved people, desperate and determined men and women who would do anything to be free. They marched throughout the day, killing more white people they encountered. Only a few whites were spared—those who had been kind to enslaved people and those who were hidden by their enslaved people. By the day's end, between twenty and twenty-five white people had been killed.

Once word of the trouble spread in the area, a violent mob of white men, armed with firepower greater than that of the rebels, descended on them. When Jemmy and his crew fired on their adversaries, they were showered with bullets. When it was all said and done, roughly thirty enslaved people had been killed. Some managed to escape, and others evaded capture for a short while before being arrested and either executed or shipped to the West Indies. Within six months, almost all those who had escaped were captured. Only one of the enslaved rebels was able to hold out longer; he managed to elude his captors for a period of three years before being captured.

Although the uprising, which came to be known as the Stono Rebellion, fell far short of white people's fears of large-scale insurrections, it did result in the deaths of sixty people, with widespread damage to plantations and other property in the area.

After the Stono Rebellion, colonists in South Carolina passed the Negro Act, prohibiting enslaved people from gathering together, growing their own food, and learning to read and write. These practices had been in effect before 1740, but the Negro Act codified them into law and established stricter guidelines for enforcing them.

THE NEW YORK SLAVE REBELLION OF 1741

While the Stono Rebellion is the only documented slave insurrection of its magnitude, and most other slave uprisings occurred in the South, many enslaved people revolted against their captors in varying degrees in the North as well. And even though slave rebellions never actually led to the overthrow of the institution of slavery, white people were horrified by what *might* happen if their enslaved people broke free of their shackles and turned the tables on their enslavers.

Sometimes enslaved people didn't even have to revolt against their enslavers for fear of mass rebellion to ensue! In the British colony of New York in 1741, a series of fires, burglaries, and false testimonies created the perfect storm for widespread paranoia, mayhem, and violence. At the center of it all was an alleged plot by enslaved people and white indentured servants to rise up against the people in charge.

On March 18, the first of several fires allegedly set by Black people spawned rumors of a planned rebellion by enslaved Black people and poor white people. An enslaved man named Cuffee, who was allegedly seen fleeing the site of the arson, was accused of the crime. A month later two enslaved people, Caesar and Prince, sold goods they had stolen from a white couple's farm to a man known for buying and selling stolen goods. While there was no evidence linking Caesar and Prince's alleged crimes to Cuffee's, the local authorities believed a conspiracy orchestrated by enslaved people and indentured servants was afoot.

As you can imagine, the pressure was on to thwart the supposed insurrection and bring the conspirators to justice quickly. But over the course of the next several months, New York City was besieged with mayhem over the fear of a mass Black rebellion!

The fear fueled suspicion of enslaved people and anyone who appeared to sympathize with them or offered them refuge from captivity. This included the country of Spain. You may be asking, What did Spain have to do with a slave revolt in British colonial North America? A lot, actually! The Spanish Crown wanted to extend its power and influence *and* that of the Catholic Church in the Americas, which meant the conversion of the various peoples they encountered and, in many instances, subjugated. Under Spanish rule, places like Florida's Saint Augustine and Fort Mosé became refuges for runaway enslaved people and newly freed people if they embraced Catholicism and fought for Spain.

Complicating matters in New York was a group of very vocal enslaved Black Spaniards who had been sold into slavery and transported to the Caribbean. By the time they reached Manhattan, they continued to voice their claims to freedom because of their allegiance to Spain and the Roman Catholic Church.

Of course, their boisterous claims didn't sit well with the white people they encountered, especially the authorities! They believed the Spaniards were a bad influence on their enslaved people and, more important, on their way of life.

A judge named Daniel Horsmanden set out to investigate the fires and burglaries and bring the criminals and co-conspirators to justice. But to do this, he needed a witness to point the finger at the accused perpetrators. To make his case, Horsmanden persuaded a young indentured servant named Mary Burton to point out Cuffee, Prince, and Caesar; Caesar's girlfriend, Peggy Kerry, who was white; and a slew of other enslaved people and white people as those responsible for the crimes and the foiled "insurrection." For her testimony in the trial, Burton was promised a reward.

As a result of Burton's coerced evidence and that of other "witnesses," who were pressured into giving false testimony, over thirty Black people—including Caesar and Prince, and four white people, including Kerry, who was pregnant at the time with Caesar's child—were publicly executed. Another eighty people, mostly Black, were permanently exiled for their involvement in the "plot."

Horsmanden documented the 1741 court proceedings in *A Journal of the Proceedings in the Detection of the Conspiracy Formed by Some White People, in Conjunction with Negro and Other Slaves,* his personal account, which is replete with "details" about the case. Today, historians suggest that Horsmanden's personal account, published three years after the case, should be taken with a grain of salt, given his swift rush to judgment and his intent to uncover a conspiracy with very little proof that one was brewing at all.

• • •

Saint Augustine and Fort Mosé

The first runaway enslaved people from the British colony of Carolina arrived in Saint Augustine, in the Spanish colony of Florida, in 1687 and included eight men, three women, and a baby. The new arrivals were allowed to stay among the Spaniards. The men were given jobs as builders and carpenters, and the women were given jobs as domestic servants, to support their new free station in life.

As word spread, Saint Augustine quickly became a destination for other runaway slaves.

Fugitive enslaved people and free Africans were afforded the opportunity to live freely in the newly established outpost if they adopted Catholicism and rejected their traditional African spiritual customs.

A rendering of what Fort Mosé looked like in the late 1730s.

Conversion to Catholicism proved advantageous for the Africans living in Saint Augustine; they were protected by Governor Diego de Quiroga when a British official sought to return the runaways to their lives in bondage in Carolina. The governor justified his action by noting their Catholic conversion, their familial ties to the area (some married and started families), and their gainful employment. In 1693, King Charles II of Spain issued the following decree:

> *As a prize for having adopted the Catholic doctrine and become Catholicized, as soon as you get this letter, set them all free and give them anything they need, and favor them as much as possible. I hope them to be an example, together with my generosity, of what others should do. I want to be notified of the following of my instructions as soon as possible.*
> **Madrid, November 7, 1693, I, the King**

It's highly probable that word of a Spanish establishment granting asylum to runaway enslaved people made its way to other slaveholding strongholds and reached the ears of desperate enslaved people in nearby territories. Pretty soon after the king's decree, Saint Augustine became a beacon of hope and self-determination for freedom-seeking enslaved people from nearby colonies like Carolina. A decade later, with the arrival of many more fugitive African slaves, Spain added additional royal decrees offering refuge and freedom for those who embraced Catholicism and agreed to four years in service to Spain. A 1733 royal decree that prohibited reimbursement to British slave owners whose enslaved people found their way to Saint Augustine included additional protection for African newcomers.

By 1738, the increasing arrivals of asylum-seeking Africans in the Spanish settlement prompted Governor Manuel de Montiano to grant them a plot of land on the outskirts of Saint Augustine to build their own settlement. There they built a fort and thatched huts similar to structures made by the Indigenous Timucua and Yamasee tribes of the region. Gracia Real de Santa Teresa de Mosé, or Fort Mosé, was the first legally established free African municipality in North America, affording them self-determination. In return, the men of Fort Mosé fought in defense of Spain by serving in the militia.

At the time of its founding, Fort Mosé was home to thirty-eight men and their families, totaling about a hundred people. This new free African community was led by Francisco Menéndez, an African and veteran of the 1715 Yamasee Wars against the Native Yamasees. The year-long conflict between British colonists and the Yamasee ended Indigenous power in the region, scattering many to Saint Augustine, where they mixed with Africans and runaway enslaved people to form a new Indigenous nation, the Seminole, of mixed-race African, Creek, and Yamasee ancestry.

In 1740, Menéndez and members of the Spanish militia fought against British forces that attacked to gain control of the Spanish colony. Governor Montiano ordered the residents of Fort Mosé to retreat to Saint Augustine for safety. The British initially had the upper hand in the fight, capturing Fort Mosé as a result. However, Spanish soldiers, with the support of the Fort Mosé militia, successfully regained control, but Fort Mosé was destroyed during the ensuing melee.

With no home to return to, the African Fort Mosé residents and other Black runaways remained living in Saint Augustine for the next ten years, when Governor Fulgencio Garcia de Solis ordered them to return and rebuild their community. Their freedom was cut short by a 1763 treaty that resulted in the transference of Florida to the British. With no other recourse available, the Fort Mosé Africans fled to Cuba alongside the rest of the Spaniards from Saint Augustine.

Today, although there isn't any physical evidence of the settlement that provided refuge for freedom-seeking African people, you can visit the site at Fort Mosé Historic State Park, where it is recognized as part of the National Underground Railroad Network to Freedom.

● ● ●

LET'S THINK ABOUT THIS:

1. How did enslaved people use their agency to resist captivity?

2. Why do you think some enslaved people believed using American laws could secure their freedom and the rights enjoyed by white people?

3. Why did Spain's King Charles II welcome runaway enslaved people to Saint Augustine and Fort Mosé?

CHAPTER 7

FREEDOM FIGHTERS, REVOLUTIONARIES, AND INSURRECTIONISTS

The colonists, early American political leaders, slave owners, and pro-slavery advocates promoted religious and pseudoscientific narratives to justify the enslavement of African people. At the same time, they praised theories about Black inferiority and savagery to justify Black servitude to white people.

By controlling the narrative about slaves—printed in books and pamphlets, and promoted in political speeches and public lectures—white leaders and elites ensured their continuous control of Black people, enslaved and free alike. Fearmongering about impending slave revolts was one way slave owners and drivers and plantation overseers justified physical discipline and constant monitoring of slave movement. For over four centuries, white historians, scientists, politicians, journalists, and creative writers have controlled the American slave narrative and what little we learned about the hidden figures whose stories rarely made it to the pages of history books.

American historical accounts have been extremely one-sided and have left most of the voices of enslaved and formerly enslaved Black people, their descendants, and free people of color silenced or relegated to the margins.

But Black freedom fighters, revolutionaries, and insurrectionists who took up arms or otherwise struck back against their white oppressors are a vital part of this nation's story.

In addition, knowing the stories of white allies is important for understanding the whole truth about slavery in the United States. White abolitionists also played major roles in helping runaway enslaved people escape slave states, avoid capture, and begin new lives in places that welcomed Black people. Many of them were deeply religious people who saw slavery as a sin in the eyes of God. Quakers, whose community is formally called the Religious Society of Friends, believe in nonviolence and peace, and they deeply opposed slavery. A core Quaker belief is that all human beings are equal and worthy of respect, so it should not come as a surprise that many Quakers aided enslaved people in their quests for freedom.

GABRIEL PROSSER

Gabriel Prosser was a twenty-five-year-old enslaved man who was the mastermind behind what would have been the largest slave revolt in U.S. history had it been successful. Gabriel was born in 1775 on a tobacco plantation in Henrico County, Virginia. He, his brothers, and his mother (who was born in Africa) were all owned by Thomas Prosser. He was described by white people who knew him as large—six feet two in height.

A drawing of Gabriel Prosser, date unknown.

Gabriel, who could read and write, was a devout Christian and was highly regarded by both white people and Black people as a born leader with a natural talent for fighting. Unfortunately, his fighting

162

skills worked against him when he got into a scrape with a white man named Absalom Johnson, from whom he and his brother Solomon had tried to steal a pig.

During the attempted theft the two men fought bitterly, and the skirmish ended with Gabriel biting off a portion of Absalom's ear. In those days, any assault of a white person by an enslaved person was a capital offense, which means it carried an automatic death sentence.

But Gabriel's life was spared! He was such a valuable worker that Thomas Prosser paid a hefty fine for his crimes, and Gabriel served only a month in jail.

Thomas Prosser made money by sending Gabriel and Solomon out to work for other white people in the area. After taking his portion off the top of what the brothers earned, Prosser allowed Gabriel and his brother to keep some of their earnings. In some places, this practice, although not widespread, allowed enslaved people to make enough money to buy their freedom or that of their loved ones. Of course, the Black wage earners still ran the risk of white people—their owners included—taking their money and keeping it for themselves. But it was a risk they were willing to take.

Gabriel Prosser's experience as hired help afforded

him a certain degree of mobility in that he could travel to other places to conduct work on behalf of his owner. While out working, he met and talked with many people. During that time, he became inspired by what he had heard about the ongoing Haitian Revolution—which had begun in 1791—and the anti-slavery efforts by the Quakers and other abolitionists.

Everything that Gabriel learned got him to thinking that the American tenets of liberty, freedom, and justice should apply to enslaved Black people. He was able to persuade somewhere between a few hundred and a few thousand enslaved people to believe the same thing. He was so persuasive that he convinced enough of them to agree to help him overthrow the white people in their vicinity and establish a Black-occupied kingdom, with Gabriel as designated king. Enslaved people from surrounding counties and cities, including Norfolk, Richmond, and Petersburg, committed to the uprising, planned for August 30, 1800.

But two incidents thwarted what might've been a large-scale insurrection. First, a thunderous rainstorm foiled Gabriel's rebellion when a footbridge was rendered impassable by the torrential rain, limiting the rebels' strategic advantage over the unsuspecting white people. Second, their plans were revealed to white slave owners by scared enslaved people who, out of fear for their owners' lives, betrayed Gabriel and his co-conspirators.

With knowledge of the planned rebellion, local white people—including the governor and an armed militia—came together to try to capture those enslaved people involved. White fear and paranoia about the enslaved rebels' intent spread quickly.

At first the co-conspirators evaded capture, but within days, thirty had been taken into custody. Gabriel Prosser and Jack Ditcher eluded capture for several weeks more. On September 14, Gabriel was captured aboard a boat in Norfolk, Virginia. He had been betrayed by a Black man seeking a reward to purchase his own freedom. (Unfortunately for him, the betrayer was paid only a small fraction of the reward advertised, not enough to secure his freedom.)

Just under a month later, on October 10, 1800, Gabriel was hanged for his role as leader of the failed uprising. When the dust finally settled, twenty-six enslaved people had been executed and many more were shipped to other states, far away from their families and loved ones. In the end, the state of Virginia paid out over $8,900 to slave owners whose enslaved people were hanged, to compensate them for the loss of their "property." Nothing was paid to those whose loved ones were executed trying to secure their freedom.

DENMARK VESEY

For almost two centuries now, Denmark Vesey has been a legendary, albeit contentious, figure among Black and white people in the coastal city of Charleston, South Carolina. Until recently, depending on whether your conversation was with a Black Charlestonian or a white one, you might have heard that Vesey was either a hero or a villain.

Like those of many enslaved people, Denmark Vesey's actual birthdate is unknown, but historians have pieced together details about his early life based on what they have uncovered about Captain Joseph Vesey, the slave trader who transported the teenage Denmark from the Caribbean island of Saint Thomas to Cape Francis, South Carolina, for sale to a slave owner there in 1781. The young Denmark's

A statue of Denmark Vesey in Hampton Park, Charleston, South Carolina.

story could've played out like those of thousands of other enslaved boys and men who spent their years enduring backbreaking work and the violent lash of slave drivers on sugar plantations in the West Indies.

But Denmark experienced severe neurological fits—most likely epileptic seizures—which diminished his value to the white man who had purchased him from Captain Vesey. The buyer insisted on returning Denmark, in the same way that you would return damaged goods or products today, and Captain Vesey was left with him as his charge.

From that point on, Denmark traveled alongside Captain Vesey on all his trading expeditions. Seeing the world and the devastating way that enslaved people were treated by white people left an indelible mark on the young man.

Some years later, when Captain Vesey settled in Charleston, Denmark would also make a name and a life for himself as a carpenter, a businessman, and a family man. In 1799, Denmark had a stroke of luck and won $600 in a local lottery. After many years dreaming of freedom, he was able to purchase his own!

Denmark's newfound freedom was bittersweet, since he could not purchase the freedom of his wife and children. His inability to provide for and protect his family was a constant reminder of the brutality and inhumanity of slavery.

Yet even with his own heartache, Denmark was a devout Christian and was very active in Charleston's African Methodist Episcopal Church, Mother Emanuel. He taught Bible classes, often citing Old Testament scriptures that depicted the persecution of the Hebrew people by the Egyptian *pharaoh,* or king, and his people. Denmark and other Black rebels who wanted to topple the institution of slavery, using the same Bible that white people used to justify slavery, fueled their listeners' burning desire for freedom and incited them to do whatever was necessary to liberate themselves from the tyranny of their white oppressors—even if that meant committing violence.

Gullah Jack Pritchard was one of Vesey's associates and his co-conspirator in one of the most famous would-be slave revolts. Gullah Jack was an African who was skilled in the folk tradition of conjure—a blend of mysticism and herbal alchemy—used in an effort to heal or protect the believer. Gullah Jack's conjure and Denmark's fiery sermons about the protective God of the Old Testament equipped them with the courage they would need to fight for their liberation and that of their loved ones still enslaved.

But Denmark Vesey and other Black Charlestonians, some free and some enslaved, also looked to the victory of Haitian Independence, the Fort Mosé refuge for runaway slaves, and even the failed Stono Rebellion for inspiration and encouragement.

Sometime in 1822, Denmark and his friend Gullah Jack began making plans to overthrow the white power structure. They set July 14 as the day they would act.

Like their Stono predecessors, Denmark and Gullah Jack knew that they would need weapons if their coup was going to work. They planned to seize weapons from local arsenals, kill the governor, and kill every white man they encountered. Then and only then would every enslaved man, woman, and child be free. But that didn't happen. In fact, nothing happened, because Denmark, Gullah Jack, and the other would-be revolutionaries were betrayed by an enslaved person who told their master everything about the brewing plot.

Within a month, Denmark Vesey was arrested. Not even a month after that, he was convicted. On July 2, Vesey, along with five of his co-conspirators, was hanged. By early August, thirty-five men in all had been hanged for their participation in the foiled uprising plot in Charleston.

Today, in Charleston's historic Hampton Park, there is a large statue to honor Denmark Vesey. And, farther into historic Charleston, there is a prodigious oak tree that stands in the middle of Ashley Avenue. Black Charlestonians call it the "Hanging Tree." Local legend says it's where Denmark Vesey and his comrades met their untimely end.

DAVID WALKER

If there were two Black men whose very names struck fear into the hearts and minds of white people in the first half of the nineteenth century in America, those men were David Walker and Nat Turner. We will discuss Nat Turner in the next section; here, we'll learn the story of the other man who threatened the system of slavery around the same time.

David Walker was a free Black man who used his business enterprise and financial means to print his fiery anti-slavery pamphlets to promote the cause of abolition. Like Denmark Vesey, Walker drew from the Bible to get his point across. He used the word of God to point out the horrors of white Christians' actions toward God's children—Black people—and also to sanction violence against their white oppressors.

Walker scared white people because he not only held bold views about abolition but also turned the tables on widespread propaganda about Black inferiority and white supremacy as ordained by God.

David Walker was born at the end of the eighteenth century in Wilmington, North Carolina, to a free mother and an enslaved father. Marriage between enslaved people was not recognized in the eyes of the law, but many masters permitted enslaved people to choose a spouse. Sometimes a free Black person married someone who was enslaved, which complicated the couple's ability to see one another as often as they liked. Ultimately, slave owners did not care about the love shared between free Black people and slaves, and they frequently broke up enslaved families by selling off a husband or wife to make a profit—or worse, as punishment for infractions.

Having parents who held two different stations in life meant that Walker lived in two distinct worlds. At that time, American law dictated that the status of children followed that of their mothers. This meant that because Walker's mother was a free woman, David was born free.

As an adult, Walker's status as a free Black man afforded him the mobility to travel throughout the country. It was during his travels that he witnessed firsthand the horrific way that white people treated

Black people—especially those who were bound by the shackles of slavery.

Eventually, Walker moved to Boston, Massachusetts, where he made a living for himself as a shop owner. There in Boston, he became an activist and writer. He joined the Massachusetts General Colored Association, an abolitionist organization, and began sharing his views on slavery and the pressing need for abolition of all enslavement in *Freedom's Journal,* the first African American newspaper. Other Black abolitionists and activists would use African American newspapers, pamphlets, and flyers to call for Black liberation well into the twentieth century.

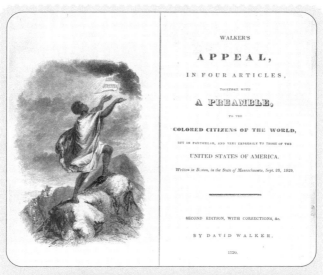

The frontispiece and title page of the second edition of David Walker's famous pamphlet. (The first edition appeared in 1829.)

Later in life, Walker channeled his feelings and observations into a series of publications. Then, in 1829, he wrote one of the most scathing abolitionist pieces of the time, a pamphlet called *Walker's Appeal, in Four Articles, Together with a Preamble, to the Colored Citizens of the World, but in Particular, and Very Expressly to Those of the United States of America.* The work was an abolitionist manifesto that gave voice to the suffering of slaves, lauded their contributions to the building of the United States, and decried the degradation and subjugation of Black people at the hands of white people who called themselves Christians:

> *Let no man of us budge one step, and let slave-holders come to beat us from our country. America is more our country, than it is the whites—we have enriched it with our blood and tears. The greatest riches in all America have arisen from our blood and tears.*

Like other Black abolitionists who used the written word to appeal to Northern white Christians, Walker used the Bible to tug at their heartstrings. The strategy was to align the modern persecution of enslaved Black people with that of the Hebrews to argue that God would surely smite those who oppressed his people.

But Walker didn't stop there! He declared that enslaved people who took up arms against their white oppressors were justified in their actions by God Almighty:

Now, I ask you had you not rather be killed than to be a slave to a tyrant, who takes the life of your mother, wife, and dear little children? Look upon your mother, wife and children, and answer God Almighty; and believe this, that it is no more harm for you to kill a man, who is trying to kill you, than it is for you to take a drink of water when thirsty.

Walker's words were so radical and controversial that many abolitionists denounced him. Nevertheless, his writings were powerful enough to incite fear among Southern white people, who believed that enslaved people could very well embrace Walker's call to arms. In 1830, for example, members of the General Assembly in Walker's home state of North Carolina banned the circulation of abolitionist material; enacted harsh penalties, including whipping and death for any Black person caught in possession of *Walker's Appeal;* and just a short time thereafter made it a crime for Black people to learn to read or write.

Walker's words were powerful! He was a prolific writer who passionately conveyed an accurate portrait of American slave culture. His words gave hope to enslaved people that freedom was their birthright—freedom could be theirs if they fought against their evil captors. Moreover, *Walker's Appeal* emphasized Black power and encouraged Black pride at the same time by honoring the great contributions and sacrifices his people had made to the United States.

It is very likely that Walker used his thriving clothing store for his covert abolitionist activities. Black sailors who traveled from the North to Southern port cities often carried news of abolition efforts in places like Philadelphia and Boston. Sometimes anti-slavery pamphlets and newspapers were slipped between the pages of local newspapers to escape detection by watchful border patrollers. Walker may have sewn his appeal into the lining of sailors' uniforms, and once they arrived in port cities like Charleston and New Orleans, the sailors would've disseminated his fiery words to slaves, free people of color, and other abolition advocates. While we don't know exactly how Walker personally managed to get his appeal into the hands of Black slaves, what's certain is that once white people caught wind of his publication, a bounty was placed on his head.

Walker was a wanted man, and the reward was not for his capture, but for his death! His friends and loved ones begged him to move to Canada, where many runaway enslaved people and free Black people had found refuge and community, but Walker was not deterred.

When he died at the young age of thirty-three, many people speculated that his death was due to foul play—namely, poisoning. But historians now believe that Walker died from tuberculosis, just as his one-year-old daughter had a few days prior.

David Walker left an enduring legacy that promoted Black pride, power, and self-determination, but more important, God-ordained self-defense against white oppressors. His words terrorized white people and inspired Black people at the same time. David Walker's *Appeal* would quicken the revolutionary spirit of Black freedom fighters well into the twentieth century.

NAT TURNER

Like David Walker, Denmark Vesey, and Gabriel Prosser, Nat Turner was a courageous Black man who used his oratory skills to galvanize enslaved people to rise up against white people in Virginia. And like Denmark and Gabriel, he was cut down by angry white people for his efforts to liberate his people.

Nat Turner was born October 2, 1800, in Southampton County, Virginia, on a plantation owned by a man named Benjamin Turner. Before he was sold, he experienced an unusual upbringing on the Turner plantation because he was allowed to learn to read, write, and study the Christian Bible. The gift of literacy and his knowledge of biblical scripture would serve him well, because he would go on to become an eloquent and persuasive preacher. Nat Turner used fiery oratory to incite a courageous willingness among his enslaved listeners to fight for their dreams of freedom.

The difference between Turner and the other freedom fighters we have discussed is that many people who knew him believed that he had been born with a special spiritual "gift" that allowed him to hear from God through visions and signs. Even as a young child, Turner claimed to receive signs from God, and he spoke with conviction and clarity about events that had taken place before he was born. The elders believed young Turner had a calling to preach and prophesy of things to come.

As an adult, Turner was an awe-inspiring preacher

who believed he had been handpicked by God to lead his followers to freedom. Through his animated preaching style, Turner masterfully gave enslaved people a new understanding of the Bible by invoking different passages than the ones that white people used to justify slavery.

Turner also believed he could see and decipher divine signs in nature. Several major events in his life were marked by occurrences of these signs. He was given a vivid vision of people whom he did not know, but whom he had seen in other visions, along with strange symbols and numbers and bloodstained cornfields. Turner took these images to mean that the liberation of his people would be justifiably won in battle sometime in the future, and that he had been preordained to lead them in their efforts to be free.

Turner remained a part of the Turner estate until Benjamin's son, Samuel, died, and he was sold to Thomas Moore. When Moore died in 1830, Turner moved to the home of a man by the name of John Travis, who had married Moore's widow.

Although Turner would later admit that believed his new owner was a "kind master," Travis and his entire family would nevertheless suffer mightily during Turner's forthcoming insurrection. After the rebellion, Turner recalled the events that led up to it:

And on the 12th of May, 1828, I heard a loud noise in the heavens, and the Spirit instantly appeared to me and said the Serpent was loosened, and Christ had laid down the yoke he had borne for the sins of men, and that I should take it on and fight against the Serpent, for the time was fast approaching when the first should be last and the last should be first. [Question.] Do you not find yourself mistaken now? [Answer.] Was not Christ crucified. And by signs in the heavens that it would make known to me when I should commence the great work—and until the first sign appeared, I should conceal it from the knowledge of men—And on the appearance of the sign, (the eclipse of the sun last February) I should arise and prepare myself, and slay my enemies with their own weapons. And immediately on the sign appearing in the heavens, the seal was removed from my lips, and I communicated the great work laid out for me to do, to four in whom I had the greatest confidence, (Henry, Hark, Nelson, and Sam)—It was intended by us to have begun the work of death on the 4th July last— Many were the plans formed and rejected by us, and it affected my mind to such a degree, that I fell sick, and the time passed without our coming to any determination how to commence—Still forming new schemes and rejecting them, when the sign appeared again, which determined me not to wait longer.

Turner and his co-rebels met one night to eat, drink, plan, and prepare themselves for the coming battle. He was joined by Hark, Henry, Nelson, Sam, Will, and Jack, all of whom were willing and ready to strike out against their oppressors.

John Travis and his entire family were the first victims of the bloody revolt. There would be more deaths to come. Upward of sixty white people were killed—men, women, and children. Throughout the night, Turner and his fellow rebels traveled from house to house, killing the white people they encountered.

Along the way, they freed the enslaved people they found and tried to persuade them to join their cause for liberation. Some joined them. Most did not, fearing what might happen if they were caught. Some tried to protect their owners. Approximately forty joined the insurrection, hoping it would end in their freedom from bondage and tyranny.

Turner and his band were headed to the town of Jerusalem, where they hoped to steal weapons for the ensuing battle. Perhaps the town's name resonated with Turner, since it was a place of significance in Jesus Christ's life. Turner believed that, like Christ, he had come to set captives free. But the rebels never made it to Jerusalem: word had gotten out about the insurrection, and a heavily armed militia of angry white men quelled their desperate fight for freedom.

Turner's rebellion fizzled into chaos, with many of his rebels being captured. Turner himself avoided capture for two months. He didn't actually get very far but was able to evade authorities by hiding in places close to the Travis farm.

Turner was eventually captured on October 30. Just five days later he was tried and convicted for his crimes. The fiery preacher who had taken it upon himself to enact the vengeance of God on white oppressors was sentenced to execution. On November 11, 1830, Nat Turner was hanged and then skinned.

When it was all said and done, fifty-five enslaved people were executed by the state of Virginia and another two hundred Black people were killed by revenge-seeking white mobs. Nat Turner's rebellion stirred up such a frenzy that even enslaved people as far away as North Carolina were accused of conspiring with Turner and his followers. They were "tried," convicted, and executed for their alleged connections to the revolt. But many of the free and enslaved Black people who were executed by the state or at the hands of local white militia had nothing to do with Nat Turner's insurrection. White people's fear fueled their desire for violent retaliation against the very Black people they had already been violently oppressing.

Over the course of Turner's final days in jail, he gave a full confession of his crimes to Thomas R. Gray, a lawyer who captured Turner's eloquence and passion and, ultimately, his justification for his actions. Even as he faced death, Turner never wavered in his belief that the violent retribution he waged against white people was ordained by God.

Nat Turner's bloody rebellion illustrates how chattel slavery bred violence at every turn and left bloody insurrection as the only option for enslaved people who could no longer endure violent subjugation for themselves and their families.

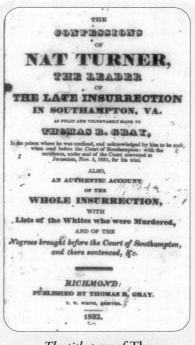

THE
CONFESSIONS
OF
NAT TURNER,
THE LEADER
OF
THE LATE INSURRECTION
IN SOUTHAMPTON, VA.
AS FULLY AND VOLUNTARILY MADE TO
THOMAS R. GRAY,
In the prison where he was confined, and acknowledged by him to be such, when read before the Court of Southampton: with the certificate, under seal of the Court convened at Jerusalem, Nov. 5, 1831, for his trial.
ALSO,
AN AUTHENTIC ACCOUNT
OF THE
WHOLE INSURRECTION,
WITH
Lists of the Whites who were Murdered,
AND OF THE
Negroes brought before the Court of Southampton, and there sentenced, &c.

RICHMOND:
PUBLISHED BY THOMAS R. GRAY.
T. W. WHITE, PRINTER.

1832.

The title page of The Confessions of Nat Turner. *Turner's words, as recorded by Thomas R. Gray, were first published in 1832.*

TRYING TO MAKE A WAY OUTTA NO WAY

There is a Southern Black saying, "make a way outta no way," which speaks to Black people's—especially Black parents'—resolve to do whatever they can to care for their children. Even during slavery, Black parents attempted to "make a way outta no way" to protect their children, including seeking their freedom through either purchase or, in many instances, death-defying escape.

By law, enslaved people were the property of their owners, which meant, in most cases, that their children also belonged to their enslavers. This had heartbreaking implications for Black parents and their children, who could be sold from one slave owner to another, miles apart, with no regard for family. For enslaved people in the North, their greatest fear was to be sold far into the Deep South—the states farthest south, where they'd be cut off from family and where slavery was much more cruel and the work more backbreaking.

Many Black families were torn apart by this practice. To make matters worse, some Black family dynamics were complicated if one parent was free while the other and the children were not. There is a Black R&B song titled "None of Us Are Free" that says, "None of us are free, one of us are chained." Written by songwriters Brenda Russell, Cynthia Weil, and Barry Mann, the song echoes the anguish free Blacks felt when their loved ones were still enslaved.

This is what a free Black man named Paul Edmonson might've felt about his family in 1848. Paul's wife,

Amelia, was enslaved in Montgomery County, Maryland, and although three of their older daughters were free, the rest of their children remained in bondage along with Amelia. Paul had been able to purchase his own freedom, and his sons-in-law had purchased the freedom of the three oldest girls. But one of the Edmonsons' sons had been sold to the Deep South when he was captured during an attempted escape.

Paul and Amelia desperately wanted their remaining children to be free, and with the help of free Black people and white abolitionists in nearby Washington, D.C., they devised a plan that, had it been successful, would have resulted in their liberation and that of over seventy other slaves. They enlisted the help of William Chaplin, a white abolitionist who facilitated the plan, which involved securing a ship to ferry runaway enslaved people from Washington to the free state of New Jersey.

They chose to depart on a Sunday since most enslaved people had Sundays off. By the time they'd be discovered missing, they'd be a long way down the Potomac River and into Chesapeake Bay. Everything was going according to plan: the crew, captain, cargo ship, and runaway caravan of seventy-one freedom seekers set off for New Jersey aboard the *Pearl* in the wee hours of April 16, 1848.

But the weather was not on their side. With

virtually no wind to propel them down the Potomac, they lingered there for most of the day before a powerful tempest forced them ashore near Point Lookout, Maryland. By this time, white residents and slave owners had set out on a steamboat to recapture the runaways and the ship's crew.

The enslaved people never even made it out of Maryland! After the ship was towed back to Washington, they were all taken at gunpoint to jail, but not before a vicious mob attacked them. Their white allies, Daniel Drayton and Edward Sayres, the captains of the *Pearl,* were taken into custody for their role in the attempted escape. The enslaved captives, including the Edmonson children, faced a far worse fate, as they were "sold south"—sent to the more terrible conditions of the Deep South.

The Edmonson girls, who had very fair complexions, were to be sold as sex slaves in New Orleans, where such practice was not only lucrative but popular among elite white men. But they were brought back to Virginia when an outbreak of yellow fever hit the port city. Not wanting to lose money over lost property, the slave traders abandoned the New Orleans enterprise altogether, and the Edmonson daughters were returned as enslaved people closer to their homes.

Hearing of his daughters' plight, their father requested the help of white abolitionists in New York to purchase the girls' freedom. The girls were emancipated in 1848. They received their education in New York State and became regulars on the abolitionist circuit, giving speeches about the horrors of slavery. Mary died of tuberculosis at twenty, having tasted freedom for only a few years. Emily went on to work alongside famous abolitionists like Frederick Douglass, with whom she helped to establish a Black enclave in the Anacostia section of Washington, D.C.

A photograph of the Fugitive Slave Law Convention in 1850. Frederick Douglass is seated at the corner of the table, with Mary Edmonson standing to his left in a plaid shawl and Emily Edmonson standing to his right, also in a plaid shawl.

While their attempt to escape by ship didn't work, their heartfelt testimonies about the brutality and anguish of slavery helped to advance the cause of abolition and therefore helped those still left behind in chains.

Colorism

Colorism is prejudice or discrimination against people of dark skin tones, including by people within their own ethnic group or "race." The term *race* is regularly used in conversation and writing to denote someone's skin color, ancestral place of origin, and or culture—but, technically, it isn't even real. The idea of race was developed by white scientists who believed that people with white skin—Caucasoid—were superior to other groups of people: Mongoloid (Asian and Indigenous American) and Negroid (or African/Black). Over time, whiteness not only equated power and privilege but also evolved to become the highest standard of beauty.

Conversely, Black people's skin, hair texture, and facial features were considered ugly.

Some formerly enslaved and freeborn Black people were so light-skinned that they could "pass" for white—pretend to be white and go undetected. They lived their lives as white people, telling no one of their real identity. Seeing the advantages that white people had, some Black people passed so that they could have better lives. Others, as you will see later, passed to save their lives.

The manifest for a ship the Edmonsons boarded in 1848, the Columbia, *which noted their color. Note Mary and Emily in rows 16 and 17, labeled "yellow," which meant mixed race.*

It wasn't until the 1960s that the Black Pride movement, which celebrated Black skin and kinky hair, took off. Yet even today African Americans find themselves in a society that celebrates and promotes white standards of beauty above all else, and there are subtle ways fairer-skinned Black people get preferential treatment, often unconsciously.

Among African Americans, colorism is rooted in slavery and European standards that do not find beauty in dark skin.

THE UNDERGROUND RAILROAD

The Underground Railroad was a sophisticated secret system for helping fugitive enslaved people make it successfully to the North. Of course, it wasn't an actual railroad that ran underground! It was a geographical network of houses, churches, sheds and barns, and secret rooms called depots and safe houses—spaces owned by courageous stationmasters and operated by equally brave conductors who risked their lives transporting passengers (runaways) from one station to the next along the arduous journey to freedom.

Conductors included both white people—men and women, wealthy people, ordinary citizens, clergymen, political figures—and Black people, including those who had been freeborn or manumitted as well as those who had escaped and lived to tell of it.

No one knows when the Underground Railroad made its first trip or who the first passengers were, but we do know that it was an outgrowth of Quaker abolitionism. The Quakers had been working to end slavery as early as the 1700s. Throughout the eighteenth and nineteenth centuries, individuals and groups of Quakers and free Black people orchestrated and facilitated clandestine plans to help freedom-seeking enslaved people get out of the antebellum—meaning the years preceding the Civil War—South. This was such a secret that it didn't have a name. In fact, whispers about the underground network didn't even surface until the mid-1830s. But by the start of the Civil War, the Underground Railroad had been operating full steam ahead!

Most passengers "boarded" in Kentucky, Virginia, and Maryland, but never in the Deep South. In order to get safe passage on the Underground Railroad, runaways from those states had to cover a great deal of their journey alone. That doesn't mean desperate enslaved people didn't get help from others who were enslaved, and in some cases from white people.

That help came from the Underground Railroad conductors—brave men and women, both Black and white—who risked their lives to help runaways by leading them to free territories. There were countless conductors who acted in secrecy to undermine slavery in the South.

The most noted and successful conductor was Harriet Tubman. After escaping enslavement on a Maryland plantation, Tubman, whose birth name was Araminta Ross, went back to get some of her relatives. In fact, the pint-sized freedom fighter made thirteen trips back into the slave state of Maryland to guide enslaved

A portrait of Harriet Tubman taken between 1871 and 1877.

people to freedom using the Underground Railroad!

By the time Tubman had taken her last run as a conductor, she had helped upward of seventy people, many of whom were her relatives. For her valor and success she was given the nickname "Moses," because like the Old Testament Hebrew liberator, Tubman led her people to freedom.

But Tubman's heroism didn't stop there! During the Civil War she served as a Union spy, providing the North with valuable information that ultimately helped in the defeat of the Confederacy and then in the emancipation of all enslaved people in 1865.

SHADRACH MINKINS AND THE FUGITIVE SLAVE ACT

Shadrach Minkins was born enslaved in Norfolk, Virginia, in 1814. He and his parents were owned by a businessman named Thomas Glenn, who operated a successful tavern in a bustling section of Norfolk.

After Glenn had died, Minkins was sold several times to settle his owners' debts. There is a saying that it is better to deal with "the devil you know" than one

SALES THIS DAY.

PURSUANT to an advertisement affixed to the door of the Court House of the city of Norfolk,

WILL BE SOLD,

At Public Auction, before the Court House, at 12 o'-clock, on MONDAY, the 23d inst.,

Negro Man Shadrach and Negro Woman Hester and her children Jim and Imogene, by virtue of a writ of fieri facias against the goods and chattels of Martha Hutchings and Edward DeCormis, at suit of Joseph Cowperthwaite, assignee of the President, Directors & Co. of the Bank of the United States.

jy 18—tds ·   WM. B. LAMB, Serg't.

(Beacon copy.)

An advertisement for the sale of several human beings, including Shadrach Minkins, 1849.

you don't know. Enslaved people must've understood this adage, fearing life might be much worse for them in a new place with new overseers, rules, routines, and physical retribution for infractions and minor missteps than the familiar, if equally awful, reality they already faced.

Minkins did not let the fear of the unknown prevent him from trying to escape! On May 3, 1850, he escaped captivity in Norfolk and made his way to Boston, which had become a haven for runaway enslaved people by that time. While there is no definitive evidence of how he managed to get there, it is likely that he traveled by ship with the help of a benevolent captain or crew members. Many successful runaway enslaved people made it to free states in the North with the help of compassionate seamen who provided safe passage.

Once he made it to Boston, Minkins ran into a friendly face: a white man he had worked with when he had been hired out to work at the R. S. Hutchings and Company grocery store in Norfolk. With William H. Parks's help, Minkins started his new life as a free man. Initially, he did odd jobs for Parks to support himself until he landed a job as a restaurant waiter at the fancy Cornhill Coffee House.

Minkins was beginning to have a good life! He changed his name to Frederick, made friends, and even joined a local church, the Twelfth Street Baptist Church. It seemed that Minkins had thrown off the shackles of slavery for good.

But that would all change as a result of the 1850 Fugitive Slave Act, which we learned about in Chapter 5. That act provided federal support to slave owners seeking the return of runaway enslaved people who had made it to free states. Local abolitionists sprang into action, mobilizing to protect fugitives who had found safe harbor in their community. Pro-slavery advocates were mobilizing as well. Slaveholders whose runaways were still at large were diligent in their pursuits of their escaped captives. They paid slave catchers, or bounty hunters, to capture and return their property by any means necessary.

John Caphart was a slave catcher notorious for his treacherous behavior in pursuit of runaway slaves. On February 12, 1851, Caphart arrived in Boston to capture Minkins and return him to the custody of John DeBree, the last man Minkins was sold to in 1849. Caphart came to town armed with official documents showing DeBree's ownership of Minkins, and the next day Minkins was taken into custody by local deputies.

When confronted by deputies and the possibility of being returned to slavery, Minkins didn't flee or resist apprehension. He was afraid and in shock.

Was it possible that he had escaped bitter slavery and finally tasted the sweetness of freedom only to have it taken away? It seemed that all hope was lost for Minkins. But then something utterly surprising happened.

After Minkins had been escorted to the courthouse across the street, scores of Black and white people crammed inside to witness the proceedings. By that time, the crowd had grown to hundreds of people in support of Minkins. A group of twenty or so Black men charged the doors and rescued the bewildered prisoner and hid him in several places throughout the city. Black activists Lewis Hayden, Robert Morris, the Reverend Joseph C. Lovejoy, and John J. Smith secured his movements to different hiding places in Boston, Cambridge, and Concord before handing him off to Francis and Ann Bigelow, who transported him to Leominster.

That was just the start of his clandestine journey! Minkins, like many other fugitive slaves, would eventually make it to freedom in Canada, outside the jurisdiction of U.S. laws, by traveling the Underground Railroad. There in Canada, he married an Irishwoman named Mary and started a family, whom he supported through restaurant jobs and a barbershop he owned and operated.

Minkins publicly thanked all those who had helped him escape in a letter that was printed in a local Boston newspaper and in Frederick Douglass's newspaper, the *North Star*. The brazen nature of Minkins's escape and the help he received from his rescuers enraged pro-slavery white people. But that didn't matter to him, because at long last, he was free!

WILLIAM AND ELLEN CRAFT

Even with the cruelty they suffered, enslaved people found reasons to be happy, occasions to celebrate, and ways to experience love. Some slaveholders allowed their bondsmen and bondswomen to marry whom they pleased. But even then there was no guarantee that a husband and wife and their children would always be together. To be in love and enslaved was a very precarious situation.

No two people knew this more than William and Ellen Craft. Their story begins in Macon, Georgia. Ellen was a fair-skinned woman, the offspring of a wealthy white planter and a mixed-race enslaved Black woman, whose own father had been her owner as well. This meant Ellen was a *quadroon:* a person who had a quarter Black ancestry. People known as quadroons were classified as Black, even when, like Ellen, they could easily pass for white.

As a child, Ellen closely resembled her father and was often mistaken for one of his white children or relatives. Ellen's likeness to her father's family angered the plantation mistress, who sent the eleven-year-old girl from Clinton, Georgia, where she was born, to Macon as a wedding present for her daughter.

William was not mixed and had darker skin than Ellen. He suffered heartbreak after heartbreak seeing his parents, brother, and sister all sold off and sent to different plantations. William learned woodworking from his master. But his owner saw him as nothing more than a financial asset, and at the age of sixteen he was put up for auction to pay off his master's debts.

William and Ellen met in Macon and fell in love. They decided to marry and were given permission to do so, even though they had different owners and lived on different plantations. Ellen worked as a lady's maid in the Big House. William worked as a cabinetmaker, and his new owner allowed him to keep a meager portion of the money he earned from his beautiful craftsmanship. It is plausible that William saved the earnings he was allowed to keep, which would eventually fund his and Ellen's courageous escape.

Like many young married couples, William and

Ellen dreamed of having a family of their own. However, they knew too well the pain of separation from parents and loved ones. They decided they would not have children while in bondage. They only had one option if they wanted the chance to have a family: run!

William and Ellen's status as "favorite" enslaved people gave them an advantage in their courageous escape. It was customary for enslaved people who were considered trustworthy or in some way special to travel between plantations or into nearby towns on errands on behalf of their masters. This privilege was an advantage William and Ellen had in their quest for freedom.

There was one major obstacle in their plan: they would need written passes from their owners saying they had permission to travel unaccompanied, but neither of them knew how to read or write.

William was struck with a bolt of ingenuity. Remember that Ellen's fair skin and resemblance to her father annoyed her original owner's wife? Well, William devised a plan that allowed the couple to take advantage of Ellen's appearance. Since it wasn't uncommon for white men to travel accompanied by slaves, William realized that the best way for them to escape without getting caught was for Ellen to don a disguise

Ellen Craft, depicted in disguise.

as a white man, with William acting as her accompanying manservant!

At first Ellen was so afraid, she didn't think she could keep up with the elaborate masquerade. But eventually, through prayer and William's encouragement, she agreed to the plan. In fact, Ellen got creative! She cut her long, soft hair just short enough to frame her face and put on some round eyeglasses to hide her feminine features. She used her sewing skills to make herself a pair of men's trousers and wore a man's jacket and top hat.

Ellen's ingenious disguise was only one part of the strategy, because they still had to figure a way to travel without official paperwork proving her "ownership" of William. The South had enacted strict protocols to prohibit white abolitionists from facilitating the transport of runaways to free states in the North, so they needed to somehow account for this in their plan. Ellen's quick thinking sprang into action. William wrapped Ellen's right arm in a sling so that she would have an excuse to avoid signing her and William's names if asked anytime during their escape.

Then there was the problem of Ellen's voice, which would be a dead giveaway that she was a woman if she was ever asked questions about their travel purpose or just approached with friendly conversation. The couple decided that the only way Ellen's voice wouldn't be a thorn in their plans was if she didn't speak at all during their escape. William wrapped Ellen's head in bandages so that it appeared "he" had a terrible toothache, which prevented "him" from readily speaking!

With Ellen's elaborate disguise and some of William's earnings, on or about December 21, 1848, the courageous couple knelt down to pray before they set out on one of the most daring escapes ever told.

William used his savings to purchase train tickets to Savannah, Georgia, and then tickets for a steamship to Charleston, South Carolina. Ellen, disguised as a white man, traveled in all-white first-class accommodations, while William had to travel in the "Negro car."

It seemed trouble followed the daring duo right from the start. Once they had taken their places on the train, William spied the owner of the cabinet-making shop peering through the train windows. As his heart sank, William slid beneath the windowsill to avoid detection by his former employer!

Meanwhile, Ellen's seatmate during the first leg of the journey happened to be a close friend of her owners who had recently eaten dinner at their house. Surely, if he had taken a close look at the "man" seated next to him, he might've discovered that "he" was Ellen, the fair-skinned enslaved woman who was the spitting image of her father. But he never did. Instead, throughout the trip, the talkative traveler tried to engage the disguised Ellen in courteous banter. Ellen had thought this possibility out too. To avoid conversation, she pretended to have poor hearing *and* a toothache so that she would have an excuse for not responding when spoken to.

William and Ellen encountered several more incidents that almost meant their demise. More than once, Ellen was propositioned with offers to purchase William, and once when she thanked William for handling her belongings, she was scolded by a white passenger standing nearby, who admonished her because such polite speech might give an enslaved man the wrong impression about his station in life.

While passing as a white traveler, Ellen experienced fine dining and the best sleeping accommodations, while William traveled amid the passengers' luggage and other cargo, as was customary for enslaved Black people accompanying their owners.

As a "white man," Ellen also ate at one of Charleston's best restaurants. There her disguise really came in handy as an excuse for not drinking and socializing with the well-to-do men she encountered.

Their escape was almost thwarted in Charleston when they encountered trouble trying to purchase steamship tickets to Philadelphia, because Ellen could not show proof that "he" in fact owned William. As luck would have it, a ship captain who had previously encountered Ellen and William vouched for the two and signed their names in the local registry, which was the custom to prevent abolitionists from absconding with enslaved people and giving them passage to free states.

In Baltimore, they again narrowly escaped detection when a border patrol officer ordered them to report to local authorities so that Ellen could prove ownership of William. Finally, after regarding Ellen's "illness" and feigned weakness, the frustrated officer relented and let the two runaways in disguise board the steamer to Philadelphia!

By the time they reached the City of Brotherly Love, it was Christmas Day. What joy and relief William and Ellen must've felt after days of heart-wrenching travel in plain sight of white people who could've apprehended and kept them as slaves, returned them to Georgia, or sold them separately to different slave owners.

There in Philadelphia they were embraced by local abolitionists, both Black and white. After three weeks they left for Boston, where they settled down, found work, and began life as free people. Safe within a welcoming environment, the couple gave vivid accounts of the horrors of slavery and details of their clever escape. Their story was the talk of the abolitionist movement, and it spread throughout free and slave states alike.

Sounds like a happy ending, right? Well, not quite yet.

Ellen's owner back in Georgia heard news of their life in Boston, and colorful details of their creative escape made it back to his plantation. And he wasn't happy one bit about William and Ellen's ability to avoid apprehension. He was on a mission to capture them.

In 1850, slave hunters arrived in Boston to

recapture the daring duo. William and Ellen had to move again. This time they were sent by boat to England, where they found sanctuary in the thriving and vocal abolitionist community there.

In England, the Crafts were surrounded by notable abolitionists and thinkers like the acclaimed author of *Uncle Tom's Cabin,* Harriet Beecher Stowe, and the Black actor Ira Aldridge. Finally, William and Ellen felt secure and safe enough to begin a family. There in England they had five children.

Twenty years later, after the Civil War had ended, the Crafts finally returned "home" to Georgia. They paid forward all that they had gained through their freedom and the kindness of their friends and supporters by opening a school to educate the newly freed Black people in Georgia.

William and Ellen were discerning and deliberate in their desire to have their future children live as free people. They could not be happy until they were free to live as full citizens. Their personal quest for freedom demonstrates their agency and self-determination. The Crafts were like other runaway slaves who went to great pains to escape captivity, in spontaneous attempts to flee, well-devised plans of escape, and complex covert operations such as the Underground Railroad in later years.

William and Ellen documented their experiences in their book, *Running a Thousand Miles for Freedom,* in which they provide details of their escape right under the noses of their white would-be apprehenders. Of course, Ellen's owner and other slave owners were incensed by their colorful narrative, which detailed how they had duped white authorities time after time!

Today there are Black and white descendants of William and Ellen Craft living in Liverpool, England; Charleston, South Carolina; Washington, D.C.; and many places in between. In recent years, their descendants from both sides of the Atlantic met and discussed their shared ancestry. Julia-Ellen Craft Davis is a retired educator who regularly gives talks about her great-great-grandparents' story.

William and Ellen Craft's great-great-granddaughter, Julia-Ellen Craft Davis, teaches fourth graders about her forebears' escape.

HOW AMERICAN NEWSPAPERS PROMOTED AND PROFITED FROM SLAVERY

For over three hundred years, Americans have relied heavily on newspapers to get the facts about local, national, and international political figures and events that affect their lives. Since the initial printing of the *Boston Newsletter*, the nation's first continuously published print newspaper, in 1704, citizens have relied on news editors, columnists, and publishers to keep them informed about the important happenings of the day.

During slavery, some newspaper publishers and writers were guilty of spreading pro-slavery propaganda and, in some instances, promoting and profiting from slavery, not only through the procurement of runaway slave ads but also by getting into the lucrative slavery enterprise.

To make money, newspaper publishers, mainly in the North, ran print ads describing the physical attributes and skills of runaway enslaved people and the rewards for catching and returning them to their owners, most of whom resided in the South. Struggling newspapers managed to stay afloat by doing business with slave owners searching for their runaway slaves. They also published ghastly accounts of slave auctions, describing in great detail the naked bodies of men and women for sale.

But they didn't stop there. Some publishers actually acted as intermediaries between slave merchants and people who were interested in buying the enslaved people described in their pages. Once a deal between the two interested parties was struck and then concluded with the sale of a captive man, woman, or child, the newspaper publisher would get his cut of the proceeds.

BLACK AND WHITE ABOLITIONISTS PUBLISHED THEIR OWN NEWSPAPERS TO COMBAT SLAVERY

Chapter 3 included a quote from Frederick Douglass about how he used clever thinking to learn to read and write. But did you know that Douglass was also a stationmaster of the Underground Railroad? Well, it's true. The home of the great orator and outspoken abolitionist was one of the stations.

Douglass used his eloquent orations to win over the white Christians he needed to take up the mantle of freedom for the enslaved. But he realized that he could appeal to only so many people at a time as he traveled from place to place to drum up support for his cause. His impact needed to be greater.

An issue of the North Star *from March 8, 1850.*

He could reach more people by publishing his personal journey to freedom, chronicled in *Narrative of the Life of Frederick Douglass, an American Slave* (1845), and through his very own newspaper, the *North Star* (1847–51). Although Douglass recognized that freedom for Black people could not be won by themselves alone, he believed in their ability to advocate for themselves and speak their truths in their own publications. And this was his impetus for starting the newspaper *North Star;* he wanted to empower his people to tell their stories freely to readers worldwide with firsthand accounts of the horrors of slavery.

Douglass wrote passionately and persuasively about the need to end slavery. Nor did he hold back his feelings about the inhumane and cruel nature of the institution. In one edition of the *North Star* he wrote the following:

> *It has long been our anxious wish to see, in this slaveholding, slave-trading, and negro-hating land, a printing-press and paper, permanently established,*

under the complete control and direction of the immediate victims of slavery and oppression. . . .

It is neither a reflection on the fidelity, nor a disparagement of the ability of our friends and fellow-laborers, to assert what "common sense affirms and only folly denies," that the man who has suffered the wrong *is the man to* demand redress,—*that the man STRUCK is the man to CRY OUT—and that he who has* endured the cruel pangs of Slavery *is the man to* advocate Liberty.

Douglass's paper featured editorials, stories, and excerpts from other Black abolitionists, including his co-editor, Martin Delany, a doctor who would go on to serve as a surgeon and then major of the Union Army's all-Black Fifty-Fourth Massachusetts Volunteer Infantry Regiment during the Civil War. The publication covered current events and also included creative work by poets and writers, including the British writer Charles Dickens and the formerly enslaved woman Harriet Jacobs, whose autobiography, *Incidents in the Life of a Slave Girl,* would be written under the pseudonym Linda Brent a decade later.

Douglass named his publication the *North Star* to refer to Polaris, the celestial body runaway enslaved people used to find their way to freedom.

Once they spotted the Big Dipper in the sky above, runaways used its location as a compass. On Southern plantations the cluster of stars that we now most often call the Big Dipper was known as the Drinking Gourd, because it looked like the hollowed-out gourd used for drinking water. Two of the stars in the Drinking Gourd are used as pointers toward Polaris, the North Star; so once a runaway spotted that constellation, he or she could find north—the way to freedom!

Douglass knew the paper's title would resonate with free Black readers and inspire those still enslaved if they ever had a chance to read it or hear about it. He embraced the written word as a powerful tool to attract anti-slavery support and as a useful weapon to wield against white oppressors. Douglass was not alone in this thinking. One of his mentors and close friends had started his own anti-slavery publication even before the *North Star* made its publication debut.

William Lloyd Garrison was an outspoken white abolitionist who, like Douglass, believed that, to be successful, anti-slavery efforts needed to appeal to the hearts and moral consciousness of white people. Garrison traveled the world speaking about the evils of slavery in hopes of galvanizing anti-slavery sympathizers and recruiting new converts to the cause of anti-slavery. He was an effective speaker and writer, and his words won him followers and enemies alike. He was more radical than Douglass: When Garrison began to advocate violence as a just means to end slavery and then denounced the U.S. Constitution, Douglass broke ties with his friend and ally.

The two men also disagreed on the need for Black people to have their own newspapers. Garrison believed anti-slavery publications like his *Liberator* served the movement's cause, but Douglass felt Black people needed their own publications to tell their own stories.

Nevertheless, Garrison continued his mission until the end of the Civil War. The *Liberator* ran from 1831 to 1865, largely with support from free Black readers, who made up roughly 75 percent of his readership.

The Black Newspaper Tradition Began in 1827 with First Publication of *Freedom's Journal*

Freedom's Journal first ran in New York in 1827, making it the first Black newspaper in the nation. The paper was the brainchild of John Russwurm and Samuel Cornish, two freeborn Black men who

EXTRACT FROM AN AMERICAN GAZETTE,

ENTITLED

Freedom's Journal.

EDITED BY A MAN OF COLOUR.

MOTTO—"RIGHTEOUSNESS EXALTETH A NATION."

SERIOUS ADDRESS TO THE MISSIONARY SOCIETIES.

YOU send Bibles and Missionaries to the uttermost ends of the earth—you compassionate the wanderers of the house of Israel—you use your utmost endeavours to enlighten the idolatrous Heathen, and to teach them the knowledge of the only true God :—nor is the rude Barbarian, or the lawless Savage forgotten.—Wherever human footsteps mark the earth, the knowledge of God is proclaimed, the Gospel preached. Your ministers daily implore the Almighty, to bless the efforts of the wandering Missionary, that through his means the Heathen might be enlightened, the Barbarian softened, the Savage tamed. The objects of your solicitude are afar off ! And are their none in this happy land, who have a claim upon your bounty, upon your compassion ? I blush for my country ! Must I tell it ? Yes : In the United States, a land blessed with a free government, salutary laws, and a delightful climate, are thousands, and tens of thousands of our fellow-creatures groaning in darkness, in bondage, and in despair.

The Bramins, Hindoos, Heathen, perish in Ganges sacred stream ; are crushed beneath the iron car of Juggernaut ; or are consumed upon the funeral pyre. They live free, and die voluntarily. Yet you think their situation deplorable, and leave no means untried to remedy it. Look in our Southern States ; you will there see a class of degraded beings, abject, miserable beyond description, who have been cruelly torn from kindred and Country, inhumanely yoked with brutes, and fettered to the soil ! These poor slaves are too low and degraded to excite compassion in the breasts of Christians ; they are not remembered in the prayers of the righteous—the light of truth breaks not upon them ;—to them the Bible is not sent ;—to their benighted souls no kind Missionary whispers words of comfort. Notwithstanding they are kept in a situation by their cruel tyrants, in which they can learn nothing but to till the soil, or to bear heavy burdens ; yet, even in this degraded state, the feelings of nature triumph over bondage ; the Slave (yes, a Slave) dares to love ; his barberous master suffers him to live with the woman of his choice :—for what ? To augment the number of human wretches, and when it is for his interest, he inhumanly tears the wife from her husband—the children from their parents : ties, that to the free, constitute the dear felicities of life, serve but to agravate their woes. The generous parent's heart is broken, when he contemplates his wretched offspring doomed to slavery from their birth ; all the ties of love, of kindred, disregarded by the lawless tyrants. I ask you, I appeal to your feelings, as men, as Christians, if there are not more objects of compassion than those to whom you send Missionaries ? The sufferings of the slaves cry loudly for vengeance ! The means are in your power to alleviate those sufferings ; will you neglect to improve those means ? Shall it be said that the Americans are less humane than the English ? Shall it be said, that you traverse the seas and the farthest corners of the earth to find objects of charity ; while the most abject, miserable race on earth, remained unpitied, unsuccoured in the bosom of your own country ? Forbid it righteous Heaven !

REDDOM, PRINTER, BIRMINGHAM.

Freedom's Journal, *volume 1,*
March 16, 1827.

wanted a publication that covered news that affected free and enslaved Black people and to provide alternative stories to the racist, pro-slavery propaganda most mainstream newspapers published.

Unfortunately, the two publishers held very different ideas about the growing colonization movement to send newly freed enslaved people to Africa (even though most had never even been to Africa), which led to the breakup of their partnership and the end of their newspaper. Russwurm was in favor of mass emigration to Africa, but Cornish and many northern free Blacks were opposed to it.

Russwurm himself eventually heeded the call for colonization and emigrated to the newly established free Black colony of Liberia.

Several years later, Cornish tried his hand again at newspaper publishing. This time he partnered with two other free Black men living in New York. Philip Alexander Bell was a writer and an outspoken journalist who began his career in anti-slavery journalism writing stories for William Lloyd Garrison's *Liberator*. Charles Bennett Ray was a vocal and noted abolitionist who championed many causes for the underserved, including advocating for the education of Black people. Together, Cornish, Bell, and Ray published the *Colored American*, which ran from 1837 to 1842. Both newspapers, along with Douglass's *North Star*, established the free Black press in the margins of American society as a place for free and enslaved Black people to get vital information and news that affected their lives.

By the time of the Civil War, there were forty Black newspapers in circulation. That number would grow substantially during the twentieth century with the migration of 6 million African Americans from the South to Northern cities such as Chicago, Detroit, and New York.

As of 2021, there were a hundred Black newspapers and corresponding online websites in the United States. The *Saint Louis American,* established in 1928, is printed weekly with a readership of 60,000. Since slavery, Black newspapers have continuously documented Black life in the United States and provided a venue for Black people to tell their stories.

Today, Black newspapers aren't the only news outlets or sources for documenting the experiences of African Americans and those of their ancestors. In fact, journalists, historians, scientists, artists, teachers, political leaders, and social justice activists of many different backgrounds are working to make sure that we never forget the truth about slavery and the making of the United States. After all, the story of American slavery *is* American history.

Slavery didn't end until 1863. Leading up to that time, the nation experienced continued division around the issue of slavery; the North wanted to end slavery, but the South wanted to keep it in place. Tensions would come to a head in 1861, when the Civil War between the North and the South erupted as a battle over slavery.

But even after the war was over and the enslaved people were freed, they weren't treated fairly by the white people who had kept them in bondage. In some instances they were treated poorly by white people in the North as well. Sometimes they were mistreated by poor white people who had very little more than they had.

Even though Abraham Lincoln's Emancipation Proclamation ended slavery in the Confederate states in January 1863—and, after the Civil War, the Thirteenth Amendment to the Constitution ended slavery throughout the United States in December 1865—discrimination against Black people did not end. Since the end of slavery, educators, politicians, activists, and students just like you continue to fight against injustices that African Americans experience that are rooted in slavery. That fight, and the fight to uncover and tell the truth about slavery, continues.

LET'S THINK ABOUT THIS:

1. What do you think was going through William and Ellen Craft's minds when they encountered a friend of her master's? How were they able to keep their cool?

2. How did colorism hinder and also help Ellen Craft and the Edmonson girls?

3. Why might African Americans have felt it was necessary for them to publish their own newspapers?

4. What types of information might Black newspapers provide that mainstream newspapers don't?

GETTING TO THE TRUTH ABOUT SLAVERY INVOLVES DIGGING UP THE PAST

Did you know that clues about the past can be found right below your feet, depending upon where you happen to be standing? By digging underground in places where historical events took place and in areas where specific groups of people may have lived, we can find evidence of people and cultures long gone. Historians, history buffs, and archaeologists alike have discovered many fascinating pieces of the puzzle of American slavery by doing just that throughout the South and North.

Through scientific and archaeological inquiry, we are actually learning more about the enslaved African people and their descendants, whose sweat, blood, and hard work laid the groundwork and built the infrastructure for American cities and whose customs and traditions helped create American culture as we know it.

Archaeological excavations are pretty cool, too! Excavations at the sites of former slave plantations, as well as in urban areas, have revealed great details about slaves—how they lived, where they slept and socialized, how they cooked, what spiritual beliefs they had, and what special items they held on to for safekeeping.

Researchers, students, and volunteers have dug beneath once-functioning farms, plantations, and estates and uncovered what life was like for enslaved people in Northern colonies like New Jersey, Massachusetts, and Maryland. Archaeological findings in these places have also revealed that large-scale plantation slavery, which we mostly associate with Southern slavery, did in fact exist there as well.

These discoveries correct the widely held myth that Northern slavery involved only small-scale slaveholding, with just a few enslaved people providing labor for small farms. They also provide tangible evidence of Black life during the colonial era. In this way, uncovered artifacts found at historical excavations offer us a glimpse of the past.

Each item is an actual remnant of slave culture. Some items found underground—below what were once plantations and farms, and in slave graveyards—include buttons, pins, shards of cookware, utensils, porcelain dolls, religious talismans, and protective amulets that help fill in the missing gaps of what life was like for slaves. More important, these remnants of slave culture provide clues about continuities in American slavery between the North and the South seldom discussed in history classes.

One such site is the sprawling Samuel Browne plantation in Salem, Connecticut, used during the colonial era. Artifacts uncovered there include remnants of sawmills; root cellars, which enslaved people used for food storage, since the cellars would be cooler than the surrounding air and prevent food from spoiling; stone shelters enslaved people may have used as living quarters; and what may have been slave burial grounds as well.

These reveal the type of work enslaved people performed there and what their living quarters could have looked like. From there, using primary sources like the *Old Farmer's Almanac* and knowledge of the building materials of the meager shacks they occupied, we can hypothesize how enslaved people may have fared during the different seasons, inclement weather, and over time in general.

One of the most shocking revelations was the discovery of a slave graveyard, which holds the remains of as many as one hundred enslaved people who were held in captivity on the Browne plantation between 1718 and 1780. These men, women, and children provided the free labor that made the Browne family rich and influential.

Merchant Colonel Samuel Browne was a wealthy land baron in Salem, Massachusetts. In 1718, he began purchasing land in what would become New Salem Parish, in the colony of Connecticut, and he would eventually own 13,000 acres. That was too much land for one man to manage, so Browne rented out some of his land to local farmers and kept 4,000 acres for himself.

Over time, Browne ran his parcel as a plantation with help from overseers to direct the day-to-day operations and supervise some sixty enslaved families who actually did the work of tilling the land. While this number is small in comparison to the numbers of enslaved people who worked on Southern plantations during the height of slavery, it is an unusually high number, given the fact that slave plantations in Rhode Island and even parts of Virginia had at most two dozen or so enslaved people during the same time period.

Like other wealthy people of their day, the Brownes were generous philanthropists, and education was an important cause they supported. Beginning in 1678, the Brownes made significant financial contributions to help establish Harvard College, including 200 acres of land and £60 (pounds sterling), today now Harvard University. This means that the oldest college in the United States was built using slave revenue.

The devastating irony is that while the Brownes actively and generously made donations to advance education for white citizens, the very people who made such contributions possible were unable to benefit from their sacrifices and labor. Harvard wouldn't graduate its first African American student until almost two centuries after the Browne family made its first donation to the nation's most prestigious college. Today the university continues to grapple with its roots in slavery by examining its archival records, making them available for research, and fostering open dialogue, educational programs, scholarships, and research funding to examine its past and encourage diversity, equity, and inclusion.

But Harvard isn't alone in its dark past. In recent years other prominent colleges and universities have unearthed secrets about some of their founders and donors who were slave owners or who used slave labor to help them amass their wealth and prestige in society, including Brown University, the University of Pennsylvania, the University of Virginia, and Georgetown University.

Connections between slavery and American colleges and universities are deeply rooted in American history and, until very recently, buried in historical records and archival papers and beneath college campus building structures.

But universities like the aforementioned ones have been doing reflective work to come to terms with their pasts by admitting to their racism. Some have established research centers and committees to further examine their institutional ties to slavery, made their slave records available for public research, and earmarked scholarships for African Americans, in some cases specifically for the descendants of those enslaved people who were owned by their founders and other donors.

SHELTER ISLAND'S SYLVESTER MANOR

Sylvester Manor Educational Farm on New York's Shelter Island, between the forks of Long Island, is a unique place, in part because even to this day it has been owned by the same family since it was established in 1651 as a *provisioning plantation,* which was a tract of land that produced food and other raw materials to be shipped elsewhere (rather than being used locally). Goods from Sylvester Manor were shipped to Barbados to support wealthy Caribbean sugar producers. Today this educational farm also offers great insights about colonial and slave foodways.

On the one hand, the enslaved people at Sylvester Manor grew their own food, which gave them the autonomy to determine what they would eat and a degree of freedom to socialize among other enslaved people during their free time. On the other hand, it was essentially an economical way for slavers to cut costs and provide even less for the people they kept in captivity and used as free labor.

In its early days, the plantation owners were part of a group of Anglo-Dutch sugar producers working together to satisfy the growing global sugar market. This consortium of sugar companies profited from the use of slave labor, as well as indentured servants and some paid Indigenous workers and Europeans, on the grounds. These wealthy businessmen grew rich from the sugar cane enslaved people chopped for elite consumption and enjoyment.

But because of excavation at the farm, we now

know a little bit more about the people whose work made sugar traders rich. From 1999 to 2005, excavations at the sprawling manor led by University of Massachusetts Boston unearthed evidence of an 8,000-acre plantation. During their digs at Sylvester Manor, archaeologists collected over a million artifacts, shards, and specimens that reveal compelling details about the lives of the people who lived and worked there and the cultures that developed over time.

ANDREW JACKSON'S HERMITAGE

An archaeological excavation at the Hermitage in Nashville, Tennessee, tells the story not only of Andrew Jackson, the seventh president of the United States, but of the enslaved people he owned who lived and worked there.

Visitors to the historic plantation can take the "In Their Footsteps: Lives of the Hermitage Enslaved Tour" to learn about Jackson's 150 or so enslaved people and the types of work they did on the plantation. The tour, however, still provides very little information about who all of them were, or where exactly each of them lived on the grounds, or what their life was like in the slave cabins, which provided meager shelter. Only three slave cabins are still standing on the property.

What we do know about Jackson's enslaved people comes from his personal documents and also from the archaeological findings of two major excavations of the property in 1974 and 2005, which uncovered twelve slave dwellings clustered in three distinct areas of the grounds.

In 1804, Jackson moved his family to the 425-acre farm that eventually became the picturesque antebellum Hermitage mansion and plantation. By the Civil War, Jackson had amassed 1,000 acres of land that would make up this impressive estate.

Excavators Sam Smith, Larry McKee, and Elizabeth Kellar, along with a team of volunteers, uncovered the building remains of a series of tiny slave dwellings that were located in what was the plantation's Field Quarter. These slave cabin remnants were made of brick, log, and wood and measured only twenty by forty feet—hardly enough room for two people, let alone a whole family!

The Field Quarter was where the bulk of Jackson's enslaved people would've lived. From these discoveries, along with Jackson's property records, we know that earlier slave cabins were constructed like log cabins, while later structures were made of brick.

Most of the slave cabins had internal pits or root cellars. But root cellars were also used for the safe-keeping of personal items enslaved people wanted to hide from enslavers, as well as protective charms, amulets, and other items carried over from African customs, rituals, and traditions they retained. The root cellars found at the Hermitage are evidence of continuities in Southern slave culture, as similar earthen storage spaces have been identified in slave dwellings on other plantations.

Archaeologists working at a construction site in Morris County, New Jersey, found structural evidence and other artifacts remaining from the Beverwyck Estate, an eighteenth-century plantation. They literally uncovered the buried history of the plantation owners and their enslaved people. Like the discoverers at the Hermitage, archaeologists unearthed clues about the enslaved people who lived there, including shackles, beads, needles, and pins, which document their enslavement and the type of work they may done on the plantation.

Recent archaeological investigations at an excavation site in Colonial Williamsburg in Virginia uncovered the structural remnants of an eighteenth-century church founded by free and enslaved Black people. A team of excavators led by Jack Gary, director of archaeology at Colonial Williamsburg, discovered the brick foundations of two structures of the First Baptist Church of Williamsburg. The team's discovery provides concrete evidence of Black colonial life and religious expression.

NEW YORK: ONE OF THE MANY CITIES THAT ENSLAVED PEOPLE BUILT

Have you ever been to New York City? Maybe you have learned about Wall Street—the global financial center for the world. Well, before it was the bustling metropolis that it is today, New York was a British colony built with the labor provided by enslaved Africans as well as free people of color.

But like much of history, this story lay covered, literally buried for centuries—until 1991, when plans for a looming skyscraper were thwarted by construction workers' uncovering bones beneath the building site. Their discovery revealed 419 African men, women, and children buried there. The African Burial Ground in Manhattan, New York, helps to document the contributions that enslaved and free Africans made to one of the most prominent cities in the world. Some of the earliest people of African descent to arrive in New York were traders from places like Santo Domingo, in what's now the Dominican Republic. Take for instance Juan "Jan" Rodrigues, a Black Santo Domingan sailor who traded regularly with the Native peoples of Manhatta—the Lenape, whom we mentioned in Chapter 1. His arrival in 1613 makes him the first documented person of African descent to come to what would eventually become New York.

Rodrigues is part of a long line of free Black seamen like Paul Cuffe, whose story is presented in Chapter 2. Other Black mariners came as fishermen, navigators, traders, and in some cases pirates. However, far more Black people eventually arrived as slave labor, used to build the city's infrastructure. Enslaved people built forts and roads. They farmed land for Dutch settlers, and they built the comfortable stone houses their slave owners lived in with their families.

Through scientific analysis of skeletal remains found at the African Burial Ground, Dr. Michael Blakey and his colleagues determined that most came from West and Central Africa, while those of later individuals indicated origin in New York. These findings, along with historical records documenting slavery in seventeenth- and eighteenth-century Dutch New Amsterdam and British New York, provide physical evidence of the people whose labor helped build what would become one of the richest and influential cities in the world.

New York City isn't the only American city to uncover the slavery in its roots. In 2013, the remains of thirty-six African men, women, and children were discovered at the Gaillard Center, a performing arts venue in Charleston, South Carolina. Construction workers unearthed the sacred resting places of the nameless people some 250 years after they had been buried. Six years later, in 2019, community residents and city officials participated in a collective memorial to honor and rebury the anonymous deceased people, giving African names to those whose final resting place had been disturbed by the construction project.

By extracting and studying gene samples and testing the DNA of the remains, researchers determined that most of the skeletons were of enslaved people who had been born in places along the coast of West Africa, but some belonged to American-born people of African descent. More than likely they were enslaved, and they had been buried between roughly 1760 and 1800. Their research also revealed that the children who were buried there had been born in South Carolina and had lived and died as enslaved people.

The United States has a history of disturbing the ancestral remains of Black and Native American people alike. The desecration of African burial grounds by the government and big corporate entities to expand local municipalities or develop prime locations for business is nothing new.

In some instances, church organizations like the Roman Catholic Archdiocese of Charleston have been the culprits of such erasure of Black lives from American history. Bishop England High School paved a parking lot on top of the graves of free Black and people of color who had been interred there as members of the Brown Fellowship Society of Charleston. Founded in 1790 as a mutual aid society for Charleston's free people of color, the organization was established to support its members' livelihoods, business enterprises, and community cohesion because they were excluded from most white organizations that did the same for their members.

Today, their final resting place is memorialized in Rivers Green at the College of Charleston, the thirteenth oldest college in the United States. In 2008, university leaders, current members and descendants of the Brown Fellowship Society, and community residents gathered to acknowledge the people who were buried there, honor them, and recognize their contributions to Charleston society and their shared history.

THE *CLOTILDA* AND AFRICATOWN

In 2019, divers discovered a long-lost piece of American history: the *Clotilda,* the last American slave ship. In 1860, a slave owner decided to take his ship to West Africa to buy enslaved people to work on his plantation, even though it was illegal to do so. Timothy Meaher didn't care about the law; he cared about having enough enslaved people to sell and to work his plantation. Once the captain had successfully unloaded the cargo of slaves, he set fire to the ship and sank what was left off the coast of Mobile, Alabama.

Some of the captives were sold off and the rest were divided up between Meaher and other men who helped fund the illegal business venture. When slavery was over, survivors of the *Clotilda* returned to the site in Mobile where they had disembarked and settled there to make a new life. Remembering their homeland and culture, the survivors called their new home Africatown.

Today the descendants of the *Clotilda* and residents are working with divers, marine archaeologists, civic leaders, and scholars to fill in the missing pieces of their ancestral story.

WE CAN USE SCIENCE TO LEARN MORE ABOUT ENSLAVED PEOPLE IN AMERICA AND THEIR DESCENDANTS

The business ledgers of slave owners provide detailed accounts about the economic impact of the slave trade but tell us very little about the victims of slavery. Very few documented the births or deaths of their enslaved people or the genealogical information of the people they kept in bondage, so we are left with missing pieces of the historical record to fully grasp everything they endured.

And while travel logs and business ledgers of slave traders, slave owners, and other writers of the time provide some details about the lucrative business of human trafficking in colonial and antebellum times, they don't paint the most accurate picture of who the enslaved people were and who their descendants became.

Today biologists, geneticists, and medical anthropologists are using DNA to fill in the gaps of understanding about the chattel enslaved people who built the United States and their modern descendants.

Let's take a look at a group of African Americans who live in, and whose ancestors occupied, what is now recognized as the Gullah Geechee Cultural Heritage Corridor, which spans the southeast coast from Wilmington, North Carolina, to Saint Augustine, Florida. Led by Congressman James Clyburn of South Carolina, the U.S. Congress established the Corridor in 2006 to recognize and preserve the culture and contributions the Gullah Geechee people made to the development of the South during slavery and after.

The Gullah Geechee people offer a unique opportunity to uncover and examine the genetic origins of enslaved Africans brought to the United States in bondage. For nearly two centuries, rice cultivation in South Carolina's Low Country was responsible for the lion's share of the state's wealth. In fact, at one point Charleston was the richest city in the country due to the agricultural production of Carolina Gold rice. The profits enslaved people's owners amassed were due to the knowledge of rice cultivation gleaned from captive Africans from the Windward Coast and Senegambia, including Sierra Leone, Guinea, and down to what is now Angola. South Carolinian planters also amassed significant wealth from the cultivation of indigo and cotton.

When these African people were forced to work together on behalf of their white captors, the first result was *cultural sharing*—the mixing of different Indigenous and European cultures, languages, and spiritual beliefs. Then came *cultural syncretism*—which, if you recall from Chapter 4, means the creation of a new cultural phenomenon when two or more different cultural elements are shared. The Gullah Geechee people of South Carolina, North Carolina, Florida, and Georgia became a new representation of the West and West Central African ethnic groups who were stolen from their homelands and brought to the port of Charleston.

Because more than 40 percent of all of the enslaved Africans who were brought to the United States came through the port of Charleston, some geneticists believe the Gullah Geechee people are a *progenitor*—ancestral—population for many African Americans. A 2021 paper by the researchers Jennifer Caldwell and Fatimah L. C. Jackson, "Evolutionary Perspectives on African North American Genetic Diversity: Origins and Prospects for Future Investigations," revealed that many subgroups of African Americans are descendants of the Gullah Geechee people.

What's even more fascinating is that Gullah Geechee people usually have less than a 10 percent ancestral admixture from non-African ethnic groups and greater African retention in language, cooking, spiritual, and cultural traditions. That means that their DNA closely resembles that of their African ancestors, with very little difference. This may help us learn more about the biological and cultural traits that make Black people a unique group of Americans.

Cracking the genetic codes of African Americans can help us unlock their ancestral pasts and help scientists determine genetic and cultural differences in what kinds of diseases people can get and how we might provide better treatments.

BLACK GIRL MAGIC: 70,000 ENSLAVED BLACK WOMEN GAVE BIRTH TO TODAY'S POPULATION OF 12.5 MILLION AFRICAN AMERICANS

Have you ever heard of Mitochondrial Eve?

She was an East African Black woman who lived some 200,000 years ago and who is considered by many scientists to be the mother of all humanity. *Mitochondrial DNA,* or mtDNA, is a genetic element that comes primarily from the eggs that women produce. While male sperm does carry some mtDNA, it is very little in comparison to the abundance found in female eggs. So mtDNA is inherited almost exclusively from the mother and is therefore inherited *matrilineally*—carried through the mother's genetic makeup.

Geneticists have learned a lot about slavery by studying mtDNA in African Americans. Remember, approximately 400,000 enslaved Africans were brought to the North American colonies and the United States and held in captivity here. Of that total population, two-thirds were males and a third were females. From this data, historians believe that a little over half of the female population, or 70,000 enslaved African women, reproduced to give rise to the entire modern African American population!

We also know that enslaved women did not have rights to their bodies, and as such, many became pregnant by Black men as well as through rape by white men. Due to their limited mobility and lack of freedom, enslaved women were forced to pair with enslaved men living on or near the same plantation, or if they were lucky, in a loving and consensual relationship with an enslaved or free Black or Indigenous man living nearby.

However, even those women who were "lucky" enough to become pregnant by mates of their choosing still had no parental rights when it came to the children they bore.

Having this DNA evidence sheds further light on how American slave culture continues to influence African American life today. For example, some researchers have looked at DNA, geography, food sources, and migration patterns to understand why African Americans are more likely than their white counterparts to develop certain chronic illnesses.

Additionally, studies that look at African American DNA and American history together, for example, have helped many African Americans understand their own ancestral pasts, including uncovering white ancestors and relatives. Examining African American genomic traits gives us concrete evidence of precolonial and colonial African existence, as well as biological links to other Black people throughout the African diaspora.

Genetics is one more piece of a gigantic jigsaw puzzle that documents the truth about African Americans and the making of the United States. But there's more. Understanding African American history can help all of us understand the truth about our nation, both the good and the bad, as well as the many buried and ignored contributions of the people who helped build it.

By amplifying the stories of four centuries of North American Black people—beginning with those free African men who arrived traveling alongside European explorers, and continuing through the hundreds of thousands of Africans forcibly brought to Southern American port cities to be sold into a lifetime of slavery, and their African American descendants—we can ensure a more accurate account of our country's historical past, celebrate the diversity of all American people, and work to make our nation a more inclusive, safe, and equitable place for all of us.

RESOURCES FOR YOUNG READERS

BOOKS

Aronson, Marc, and Marina Budhos. *Sugar Changed the World: A Story of Magic, Spice, Slavery, Freedom, and Science.* New York: Clarion Books, 2010.

Barden, Cindy. *Slavery, Civil War, and Reconstruction, Grades 6–12.* American History Series. Quincy, IL: Mark Twain Media, 2011.

Conkling, Winifred. *Passenger on the Pearl: The True Story of Emily Edmonson's Flight from Slavery.* Chapel Hill, NC: Algonquin Young Readers, 2015.

Dunbar, Erica Armstrong, and Kathleen Van Cleve. *Never Caught, the Story of Ona Judge: George and Martha Washington's Courageous Slave Who Dared to Run Away.* Young Readers Edition. New York: Aladdin, 2019.

Equiano, Olaudah. *The Interesting Narrative and Other Writings,* rev. ed. New York: Penguin Books, 2003.

Hale, Nathan. *The Underground Abductor: An Abolitionist Tale About Harriet Tubman.* Nathan Hale's Hazardous Tales 5. New York: Amulet Books, 2015.

Jacobs, Harriet. *Incidents in the Life of a Slave Girl.* Mineola, NY: Dover Publications, 2001.

Myers, Laurie. *Escape by Night: A Civil War Adventure.* New York: Square Fish, 2014.

Pesci, David. *Amistad: The Thunder of Freedom.* New York: Da Capo Press, 1997.

Sterne, Emma Gelders. *The Story of the Amistad.* Mineola, NY: Dover Publications, 2001.

WEBSITES

African Burial Ground, National Park Service: nps.gov/afbg/index.htm

Amistad Research Center: amistadresearchcenter.org

The Avery Research Center for African American History and Culture: avery.cofc.edu

Fort Mose Historic State Park, Florida State Parks: floridastateparks.org /parks-and-trails/fort-mose-historic-state-park

Grand Central Station of the Underground Railroad, Indiana State Museum and Historic Sites: indianamuseum.org/historic-sites/levi-catharine-coffin-house

Harriet Tubman Museum of New Jersey: harriettubmanmuseum.org

Harriet Tubman Underground Railroad Byway: harriettubmanbyway.org /harriet-tubman

International Slavery Museum, National Museums Liverpool: liverpoolmuseums.org .uk/international-slavery-museum

Monticello: monticello.org

National Museum of African American History and Culture, Smithsonian: nmaahc.si.edu

Old Slave Mart Museum: oldslavemartmuseum.com

Path to Freedom on Illinois' Underground Railroad, Enjoy Illinois: enjoyillinois.com /travel-illinois/illinois-underground-railroad

Penn Center: penncenter.com

BIBLIOGRAPHY

2018 Global Slavery Index. Walk Free. globalslaveryindex.org/2018/findings
/regional-analysis/arab-states/.

"A 19th Century Slave Diet." National Park Service. nps.gov/bowa/learn
/historyculture/upload/THE-FINAL-Slave-Diet-site-bulletin.pdf.

Adams, T. H. "Washington's Runaway Slave, and How Portsmouth Freed Her,"
Granite (NH) Freeman, May 22, 1845, reprinted in *Frank W. Miller's New Hampshire
Portsmouth Weekly,* June 2, 1877.

"African Burial Ground in History." African Burial Ground National Monument.
National Park Service. Updated January 31, 2023. nps.gov/afbg/learn/historyculture
/african-burial-ground-in-history.htm.

"Africans in Colonial America." National Geographic Society. May 20, 2022.
education.nationalgeographic.org/resource/africans-colonial-america.

"African Americans in St. Augustine 1565–1821." National Park Service. nps.gov/casa
/learn/historyculture/african-americans-in-st-augustine-1565-1821.htm.

"A Journey in Chains." Library of Congress. loc.gov/classroom-materials/immigration
/african/journey-in-chains/.

"Amerigo Vespucci." History.com. November 9, 2009, updated November 2, 2018.
history.com/topics/exploration/amerigo-vespucci.

"Beginnings: Exploration and Colonization." Library of Congress. loc.gov
/classroom-materials/immigration/african/beginnings/.

Berlin, Ira. *Many Thousands Gone: The First Two Centuries of Slavery in North America.*
Cambridge, MA: Belknap Press, 2000.

———.*Generations of Captivity: A History of African-American Slaves.* Cambridge, MA:
Belknap Press, 2004.

"Biography." paulcuffe.org/biography/.

Blassingame, John W. *The Slave Community: Plantation Life in the Antebellum South.*
New York: Oxford University Press, 1979.

Bourne, Joel K., Jr. "Digging for the Life Stories of Long-Forgotten Slaves."
National Geographic, December 11, 2018. nationalgeographic.com/culture/article
/charleston-gullah-dna-anson-slave-burials.

Braly, Anne. "Soul Food: From the Trauma of Slavery Came Beautiful Cuisine."
Tennessee Lookout, June 19, 2020. tennesseelookout.com/2020/06/19
/soul-food-from-the-trauma-of-slavery-came-beautiful-cuisine/.

Brockell, Gillian. "The African Roots of Inoculation in America: Saving Lives for
Three Centuries." *Washington Post,* December 15, 2020. washingtonpost.com
/history/2020/12/15/enslaved-african-smallpox-vaccine-coronavirus/.

———. "Desperate for Freedom, 77 Enslaved People Tried to Escape Aboard the *Pearl.*

They Almost Made It." *Philadelphia Tribune,* April 23, 2021. phillytrib.com/news
/across_america/desperate-for-freedom-77-enslaved-people-tried-to-escape-aboard
-the-pearl-they-almost-made/article_6b8739b3-22d6-5dad-b050-6f191a95ce6c.html.

Chaidez, Alexandra. "How an Enslaved Man Helped Boston Battle a Devastating
Disease 300 Years Ago." NBC Boston. February 26, 2021. nbcboston.com/news
/local/how-an-enslaved-man-helped-boston-battle-a-devastating-disease-300-years
-ago/2300728/.

Chervinsky, Lindsay M. "The Enslaved Household of President George Washington."
The White House Historical Association. September 6, 2019. whitehousehistory.org
/the-enslaved-household-of-president-george-washington.

———. "The Remarkable Story of Ona Judge." The White House Historical
Association. October 21, 2019. whitehousehistory.org/the-remarkable
-story-of-ona-judge.

"Compromise of 1850." History.com. October 27, 2009, updated February 10, 2020.
history.com/topics/slavery/compromise-of-1850.

Craft, William, and Ellen Craft. *Running a Thousand Miles to Freedom: The Escape of
William and Ellen Craft from Slavery.* Athens, GA: University of Georgia Press, 1999.

"David Walker, 1796–1830." *Africans in America, Part 4.* PBS Thirteen. pbs.org/wgbh
/aia/part4/4p2930.html.

Desikan, Anita. "Confronting Smallpox: How an Enslaved Man Helped Spur the First
US Vaccine Study." Union of Concerned Scientists. February 1, 2022. blog.ucsusa
.org/anita-desikan/confronting-smallpox-how-an-enslaved-man-helped-spur-the
-first-us-vaccine-study/.

"Discovering the Legacy of African Cultures." Gullah Geechee Cultural Heritage
Corridor Commission. Accessed January 20, 2023. gullahgeecheecorridor.org.

"Elizabeth Freeman (Mum Bett)." *Africans in America, Part 2.* PBS Thirteen. pbs.org
/wgbh/aia/part2/2p39.html.

"Enslaved Families of Monticello." Monticello.org. Accessed January 24, 2023.
monticello.org/slavery/paradox-of-liberty/enslaved-families-of-monticello/.

"Enslaved Household of President George Washington—Photo 1." The White House
Historical Association. Accessed January 24, 2023. whitehousehistory.org/photos
/the-enslaved-household-of-president-george-washington-photo-1.

Farrow, Anne, Joel Lang, and Jenifer Frank. *Complicity: How the North Promoted,
Prolonged, and Profited from Slavery.* New York: Ballantine Books, 2006.

Fofana, Dalla Malé. "Senegal, the African Slave Trade, and the Door of No Return:
Giving Witness to Gorée Island." *Humanities* 9 (3): 57. July 2, 2020.
doi.org/10.3390/h9030057.

"Fort Mose." Florida Museum of Natural History. floridamuseum.ufl.edu/exhibits
/online/fort-mose/.

"Frederick Douglass Newspapers, 1847 to 1874." Library of Congress. loc.gov
/collections/frederick-douglass-newspapers/about-this-collection/.

"From George Washington to Oliver Wolcott, 1 September 1796." *Founders Online.*
National Archives. founders.archives.gov/documents/Washington/05-20-02-0397.

"From Thomas Jefferson to David Hartley, 2 July 1787." *Founders Online.* National
Archives. founders.archives.gov/documents/Jefferson/01-11-02-0441.

Gates, Henry Louis, Jr. "Who Led the First Back-to-Africa Effort?" The African
Americans: Many Rivers to Cross. Originally posted on *The Root.* pbs.org
/wnet/african-americans-many-rivers-to-cross/history/who-led-the-1st
-back-to-africa-effort/.

"General Court Responds to Runaway Servants and Slaves (1640)."
Encyclopedia Virginia. Virginia Humanities. encyclopediavirginia.org/entries
/general-court-responds-to-runaway-servants-and-slaves-1640/.

Genovese, Eugene D. *Roll, Jordan, Roll: The World the Slaves Made.* New York: Vintage
Books, 1976.

Goodell, William. *The American Slave Code in Theory and Practice: Its Distinctive
Features Shown by Its Statutes, Judicial Decisions, and Illustrative Facts.* New York:
American and Foreign Anti-Slavery Society, 1853.

Hayford, Vanessa. "The Humble History of Soul Food." Black Foodie. January 22,
2018. blackfoodie.co/the-humble-history-of-soul-food/.

Hinks, Peter P. *To Awaken My Afflicted Brethren: David Walker and the Problem
of Antebellum Slave Resistance.* University Park, PA: Pennsylvania State University
Press, 2010.

Hobbs, Stephen. "Tears and Celebration Mark Charleston Reburial of Skeletal Remains
of 36 People." *Post and Courier* (Charleston, SC), May 4, 2019. postandcourier.com
/news/tears-and-celebration-mark-charleston-reburial-of-skeletal-remains-of-36
-people/article_1fbabaa4-6774-11e9-a624-3f897829437b.html.

" 'I Will Be Heard!' Abolitionism in America." Cornell University Division of Rare and
Manuscript Collections. rmc.library.cornell.edu/abolitionism/narratives.htm.

Jahannes, Naftal. "Black Influences Have Shaped American Food for Centuries."
Savannah Morning News, February 22, 2021. savannahnow.com/story/lifestyle/2021
/02/22/africans-brought-different-seeds-and-plants-americas/4505785001/.

"James Armistead Lafayette." American Battlefield Trust. battlefields.org/learn
/biographies/james-armistead-lafayette.

"Juan Garrido." National Park Service. nps.gov/people/juargarrido.htm.

Kelly, William. "Slavery and Strategy in Decatur House." The White House Historical
Association. June 7, 2022. whitehousehistory.org/slavery-and-strategy-in-decatur-house.

King, Gilbert. "The Day Henry Clay Refused to Compromise." *Smithsonian Magazine,*
December 6, 2012. smithsonianmag.com/history/the-day-henry-clay-refused-to
-compromise-153589853/.

Kolo, Catherine. "Slave Marriage, Free Marriage: Black Veterans and Their Families
After the Civil War." University of Virginia, John L. Nau III Center for Civil War
History. August 4, 2020. naucenter.as.virginia.edu/slave-marriage-free-marriage.

Lang, Joel. "Chapter One: The Plantation Next Door." *Hartford Courant,* September
29, 2002. courant.com/news/special-reports/hc-plantation.artsep29-story.html.

Lech, Kristen. "Slavery in Colonial America." Study.com. Working Scholars. Updated
January 16, 2022. study.com/learn/lesson/slavery-in-the-colonies-history-overview
.html.

Mark, Joshua J. "Slavery in Colonial America." World History Encyclopedia. April 22,
2021. worldhistory.org/article/1739/slavery-in-colonial-america/.

"Mumbet and Agrippa Hull." Elizabeth Freeman. elizabethfreeman.mumbet.com
/who-is-mumbet/mumbet-and-agrippa-hull/.

"Mumbet's Grave." Elizabeth Freeman. elizabethfreeman.mumbet.com
/who-is-mumbet/mumbets-grave/.

"New York Slave Rebellion of 1741." *Encyclopaedia Britannica.* britannica.com/event
/New-York-slave-rebellion-of-1741.

O'Neil, Aaron. "Estimated Number of Slaves Taken from Africa by Region
1501–1866." Statista. June 21, 2022. statista.com/statistics/1150475
/number-slaves-taken-from-africa-by-region-century/.

242

"Our History." Sylvester Manor. Accessed January 20, 2023. sylvestermanor.org
/history.

Patton, Stacey. "Corporal Punishment in Black Communities: Not an Intrinsic
Cultural Tradition but Racial Trauma." American Psychological Association. April
2017. apa.org/pi/families/resources/newsletter/2017/04/racial-trauma.

Pavlu, George. "Recalling Africa's Harrowing Tale of Its First Slavers—the Arabs—as
UK Slave Trade Abolition Is Commemorated." NewAfrican, March 27, 2018.
newafricanmagazine.com/16616/.

Pruitt, Sarah. "What Part of Africa Did Most Enslaved People Come From?"
History.com. May 3, 2016, updated April 25, 2022. history.com/news
/what-part-of-africa-did-most-slaves-come-from.

Rediker, Marcus. The Slave Ship: A Human History. New York: Penguin Books, 2008.

Serena, Katie. "How Madame LaLaurie Turned Her New Orleans Mansion into a
House of Horrors." All That's Interesting. October 5, 2021, updated October 20,
2021. allthatsinteresting.com/madame-lalaurie.

"Slavery and Law in 17th Century Massachusetts." National Park Service. nps.gov
/articles/000/slavery-and-law-in-early-ma.htm.

"Slavery and the Making of America. The Slave Experience: Responses to
Enslavement." Thirteen/WNET New York. 2004. thirteen.org/wnet/slavery
/experience/responses/spotlight.html.

"Slavery at Monticello." Monticello.org. monticello.org/slavery/.

"Slavery in America." History.com. November 12, 2009, updated February 7, 2023.
history.com/topics/black-history/slavery.

Smith, Candace, Aude Soichet, Jessica Hopper, Ashley Riegle, and Marlene Lenthang.
"Black Americans Reconnect with Roots in Emotional Trips to Ghana's 'Door of No
Return.'" ABC News Network. February 26, 2021. abcnews.go.com/International
/black-americans-reconnect-roots-emotional-trips-ghanas-door/story?id=76122759.

Stampp, Kenneth M. The Peculiar Institution: Slavery in the Ante-Bellum South. New
York: Vintage, 1956, 1989.

Szalay, Jessie, and Callum McKelvie. "Amerigo Vespucci: Italian Explorer Who Named
America." Live Science. Updated February 9, 2022. livescience.com/42510-amerigo
-vespucci.html.

Sutherland, Claudia. "Stono Rebellion (1739)." Blackpast. September 18, 2018.
blackpast.org/african-american-history/stono-rebellion-1739.

"The Constitution of the United States: A Transcription." America's Founding
Documents. National Archives. archives.gov/founding-docs/constitution-transcript.

"The John Punch Court Decisions and the Advent of Slavery in Virginia." American
Evolution: Virginia to America 1619–2019. americanevolution2019.com/wp-content
/uploads/2018/08/PDF-The-John-Punch-Court-Decisions-and-the-Advent-of
-Slavery-in-Virginia-Full-Lesson.pdf.

"The King's Edict." The Mound Project and Other Miami Tales. hiddenhistorymiami
.com/the-kings-edict/.

"The Life of Sally Hemings." Monticello.org. monticello.org/sallyhemings/.

"The Trans-Atlantic Slave Trade." African Passages, Low-Country Adaptations. Low-
Country Digital History Initiative. ldhi.library.cofc.edu/exhibits/show
/africanpassageslowcountryadapt/introductionatlanticworld
/trans_atlantic_slave_trade.

"This Day in History, April 10, 1834: A Torture Chamber Is Uncovered by Arson."

History.com. November 13, 2009, updated April 8, 2020. history.com
/this-day-in-history/a-torture-chamber-is-uncovered-by-arson.

"Thomas Jefferson and Sally Hemings: A Brief Account." Monticello.org. monticello.org
/thomas-jefferson/jefferson-slavery/thomas-jefferson-and-sally-hemings-a-brief-account/.

"Virginia Recognizes Slavery." *Africans in America, Part 1.* PBS Thirteen. pbs.org
/wgbh/aia/part1/1p262.html.

Walker, David. *David Walker's Appeal, in Four Articles: Together with a Preamble to the
Coloured Citizens of the World, but in Particular, and Very Expressly, to Those of the
United States of America.* Revised edition with an Introduction by Sean Wilentz. New
York: Hill and Wang, 1995.

Wheatley, Phillis. Phillis Wheatley to Mary Wooster. Collection of the Massachusetts
Historical Society. Boston, MA, July 15, 1778.

Wilkinson, Freddie. "New England Colonies' Use of Slavery." National Geographic
Resource Library. June 2, 2022. education.nationalgeographic.org/resource
/new-england-colonies-use-slaves.

Wood, Peter H. *Black Majority: Negroes in Colonial South Carolina from 1670 through
the Stono Rebellion.* New York: W. W. Norton, 1975.

IMAGE CREDITS